STRENGTHENING PEER REVIEW IN FEDERAL AGENCIES THAT SUPPORT EDUCATION RESEARCH

Committee on Research in Education

Lisa Towne, Jack M. Fletcher, and Lauress L. Wise, Editors

Center for Education

Division of Behavioral and Social Sciences and Education

NATIONAL RESEARCH COUNCIL
OF THE NATIONAL ACADEMIES

THE NATIONAL ACADEMIES PRESS
Washington, D.C.
www.nap.edu

THE NATIONAL ACADEMIES PRESS   500 Fifth Street, N.W.   Washington, DC 20001

NOTICE: The project that is the subject of this report was approved by the Governing Board of the National Research Council, whose members are drawn from the councils of the National Academy of Sciences, the National Academy of Engineering, and the Institute of Medicine. The members of the committee responsible for the report were chosen for their special competences and with regard for appropriate balance.

This study was supported by Contract No. ED-00-CO-0088 between the National Academy of Sciences and the U.S. Department of Education, Grant No. 2002-7860 from the William and Flora Hewlett Foundation, and Grant No. 200200225 from the Spencer Foundation. Any opinions, findings, conclusions, or recommendations expressed in this publication are those of the authors and do not necessarily reflect the views of the U.S. Department of Education, the William and Flora Hewlett Foundation, or the Spencer Foundation.

International Standard Book Number 0-309-09099-7(Book)
International Standard Book Number 0-309-52814-3 (PDF)

Additional copies of this report are available from National Academies Press, 500 Fifth Street, N.W., Lockbox 285, Washington, DC 20055; (800) 624-6242 or (202) 334-3313 (in the Washington metropolitan area); Internet, http://www.nap.edu

Printed in the United States of America

Copyright 2004 by the National Academy of Sciences. All rights reserved.

Suggested citation: National Research Council. (2004). *Strengthening Peer Review in Federal Agencies That Support Education Research*. Committee on Research in Education. L. Towne, J.M. Fletcher, and L.L. Wise, Eds. Center for Education, Division of Behavioral and Social Sciences and Education. Washington, DC: The National Academies Press.

THE NATIONAL ACADEMIES
Advisers to the Nation on Science, Engineering, and Medicine

The **National Academy of Sciences** is a private, nonprofit, self-perpetuating society of distinguished scholars engaged in scientific and engineering research, dedicated to the furtherance of science and technology and to their use for the general welfare. Upon the authority of the charter granted to it by the Congress in 1863, the Academy has a mandate that requires it to advise the federal government on scientific and technical matters. Dr. Bruce M. Alberts is president of the National Academy of Sciences.

The **National Academy of Engineering** was established in 1964, under the charter of the National Academy of Sciences, as a parallel organization of outstanding engineers. It is autonomous in its administration and in the selection of its members, sharing with the National Academy of Sciences the responsibility for advising the federal government. The National Academy of Engineering also sponsors engineering programs aimed at meeting national needs, encourages education and research, and recognizes the superior achievements of engineers. Dr. Wm. A. Wulf is president of the National Academy of Engineering.

The **Institute of Medicine** was established in 1970 by the National Academy of Sciences to secure the services of eminent members of appropriate professions in the examination of policy matters pertaining to the health of the public. The Institute acts under the responsibility given to the National Academy of Sciences by its congressional charter to be an adviser to the federal government and, upon its own initiative, to identify issues of medical care, research, and education. Dr. Harvey V. Fineberg is president of the Institute of Medicine.

The **National Research Council** was organized by the National Academy of Sciences in 1916 to associate the broad community of science and technology with the Academy's purposes of furthering knowledge and advising the federal government. Functioning in accordance with general policies determined by the Academy, the Council has become the principal operating agency of both the National Academy of Sciences and the National Academy of Engineering in providing services to the government, the public, and the scientific and engineering communities. The Council is administered jointly by both Academies and the Institute of Medicine. Dr. Bruce M. Alberts and Dr. Wm. A. Wulf are chair and vice chair, respectively, of the National Research Council.

www.national-academies.org

COMMITTEE ON RESEARCH IN EDUCATION
2004

Lauress L. Wise (*Chair*), Human Resources Research Organization (HumRRO), Arlington, VA
Linda Chinnia, Baltimore City Public School System
Kay Dickersin, Department of Community Health, Brown University
Margaret Eisenhart, School of Education, University of Colorado, Boulder
Karen Falkenberg, Division of Educational Studies, Emory University
Jack McFarlin Fletcher, University of Texas-Houston Health Science Center and Center for Academic and Reading Skills
Robert E. Floden, College of Education, Michigan State University
Ernest M. Henley (emeritus), Department of Physics, University of Washington
Vinetta C. Jones, School of Education, Howard University
Brian W. Junker, Department of Statistics, Carnegie Mellon University
David Klahr, Department of Psychology, Carnegie Mellon University
Ellen Condliffe Lagemann, Harvard Graduate School of Education
Barbara Schneider, Department of Sociology, University of Chicago
Joseph Tobin, College of Education, Arizona State University

Lisa Towne, *Study Director*
Tina Winters, *Research Associate*

Preface

The central idea of evidence-based education—that education policy and practice ought to be fashioned based on what is known from rigorous research—offers a compelling way to approach reform efforts. Recent federal trends reflect a growing enthusiasm for such change. Most visibly, the No Child Left Behind Act of 2001 requires that "scientifically based [education] research" drive the use of federal education funds at the state and local levels. This emphasis is also reflected in a number of government and nongovernment initiatives across the country. As consensus builds around the goals of evidence-based education, consideration of what it will take to make it a reality becomes the crucial next step.

In this context, the Center for Education of the National Research Council (NRC) has undertaken a series of activities to address issues related to the quality of scientific education research.[1] In 2002, the NRC released *Scientific Research in Education* (National Research Council, 2002), a report designed to articulate the nature of scientific education research and to guide efforts aimed at improving its quality. Building on this work, the Committee on Research in Education was convened to advance an improved understanding of a scientific approach to addressing education prob-

---

[1] Other NRC efforts—especially the line of work that culminated in the recent report *Strategic Education Research Partnership* (National Research Council, 2003)—offer insights and advice about ways to advance research utilization more broadly.

lems; to engage the field of education research in action-oriented dialogue about how to further the accumulation of scientific knowledge; and to coordinate, support, and promote cross-fertilization among NRC efforts in education research.

The main locus of activity undertaken to meet these objectives was a year-long series of workshops to engage a range of education stakeholders in discussions about five key topics:

• *Peer Review in Federal Education Research Programs.* This workshop focused on the purposes and practices of peer review in the federal agencies that fund education research. Federal officials and researchers considered a range of models used across the federal government to involve peers in the review of proposals for funding and discussed ways to foster high-quality scientific research.

• *Understanding and Promoting Knowledge Accumulation in Education: Tools and Strategies for Education Research.* With a focus on how to build a coherent knowledge base in education research, researchers and federal officials considered several elements of the research infrastructure, including tools, practices, models, and standards. Fundamental questions about what such a knowledge base might look like were also considered in this context.

• *Random Assignment Experimentation in Education: Implementation and Implications.* The evidence-based education trend has brought to the fore decades of debate about the appropriateness of randomized field trials in education. Far less consideration has been devoted to the practical aspects of conducting such studies in educational settings; this workshop featured detailed descriptions of studies using randomized field trials in education and reflections on how the current trend to fund more of these studies is influencing states, districts, and students.

• *Journal Practices in Publishing Education Research.* Following the more general discussion of how to build a coherent knowledge base in education in a previous workshop, this event took up the specific case of journals that publish education research. Editors, publication committee members, and others involved in the production and use of journal articles considered ways to promote high-quality education research and to contribute to the larger body of knowledge about important areas of policy and practice.

• *Education Doctoral Programs for Future Leaders in Education Research.* A final workshop focused on the professional development of education researchers, with a specific emphasis on doctoral programs in schools of education. Deans, graduate study coordinators, foundation officials, and policy makers came together to share observations and chart potential paths for progress.

Additional information on each of these events can be found at http://www7.nationalacademies.org/core/.

This report is based on the first workshop in the series, on peer review in federal agencies that support education research, which took place on February 25-26, 2003, at the National Academies' Keck Center in Washington, DC. It summarizes common issues and ideas that emerged from the presentations and discussion during the workshop (see Appendix A for the workshop agenda and Appendix B for biographical sketches of the committee members and speakers) and includes the committee's conclusions and recommendations on how to strengthen peer review in federal agencies that support education research.

This report would not have been possible without the help of the speakers who shared their expertise with the committee. We would like to thank each of them for their contributions:

Diane August, August and Associates; Hilda Borko, University of Colorado, Boulder; Steven Breckler, National Science Foundation; Susan Chipman, Office of Naval Research; Domenic Cicchetti, Yale University; Louis Danielson, Office of Special Education Programs; Kenneth Dodge, Duke University; Edward Hackett, Arizona State University; Milton Hakel, Bowling Green State University; Teresa Levitin, National Institutes of Health; Penelope Peterson, Northwestern University; Edward Reddish, University of Maryland; Finbarr Sloane, National Science Foundation; Brent Stanfield, National Institutes of Health; Robert Sternberg, Yale University; and Grover (Russ) Whitehurst, Institute of Education Sciences.

Of course, without the generous support of our sponsors, neither the workshop nor this report would be possible. We extend our gratitude to the former National Educational Research Policy and Priorities Board and the Institute of Education Sciences, the William and Flora Hewlett Foundation, and the Spencer Foundation.

We extend our thanks to each of the members of the Committee on Research in Education. We especially appreciate the efforts of the workshop planning group, led by Jack Fletcher, who designed an outstanding event that has made a unique contribution to an important debate. Several

NRC staff played critical roles in shaping the workshop and deserve special recognition here: Meryl Bertenthal led the staff effort, substantively supported by Tina Winters. R. Jason Rolsen provided the administrative and logistical support for the committee as well as for the event itself. And Patricia Morison offered general direction and guidance. Finally, we thank Chris McShane for her skillful editing of the manuscript.

This report has been reviewed in draft form by individuals chosen for their diverse perspectives and technical expertise, in accordance with procedures approved by the NRC's Report Review Committee. The purpose of this independent review is to provide candid and critical comments that will assist the institution in making its published report as sound as possible and to ensure that the report meets institutional standards for objectivity, evidence, and responsiveness to the study charge. The review comments and draft manuscript remain confidential to protect the integrity of the deliberative process.

We wish to thank the following individuals for their review of this report: Michael Allen, Teaching Quality Policy Center, Education Commission of the States; Rolf Blank, Education Indicators, Council of Chief State School Officers; Hilda Borko, School of Education, University of Colorado, Boulder; Robert Crangle, President, Rose & Crangle, Ltd., Lincoln, KS; Daniel L. Goroff, Department of Mathematics; and Derek Bok Center for Teaching and Learning, Harvard University.

Although the reviewers listed above have provided many constructive comments and suggestions, they were not asked to endorse the conclusions or recommendations, nor did they see the final draft of the report before its release. The review of this report was overseen by Norman Hackerman, Scientific Advisory Board, The Robert A. Welch Foundation, Houston, TX and Department of Chemistry and Biochemistry (emeritus), The University of Texas at Austin. Appointed by the NRC, he was responsible for making certain that an independent examination of this report was carried out in accordance with institutional procedures and that all review comments were carefully considered. Responsibility for the final content of this report rests entirely with the authoring committee and the institution.

Lauress L. Wise, *Chair*
Lisa Towne, *Study Director*
Committee on Research in Education

Contents

EXECUTIVE SUMMARY ... 1
   Identifying and Supporting High-Quality Research, 2
   Further Developing a Professional Culture of Inquiry, 5
   Agency Management and Infrastructure, 7
   Conclusion, 8

1 SETTING THE STAGE ... 9
   A Tool of U.S. Science Policy, 9
   Policy Context, 11
   Implications and Themes, 14
   Sources of Evidence, 15
   Objective and Approach, 17
   Organization of Report, 19

2 ANALYZING KEY ELEMENTS ... 20
   Multiple Purposes and Values, 21
   Key Objectives of Peer Review for Education Research, 24
   Identifying and Supporting High-Quality Research, 27
   Further Developing a Professional Culture of Inquiry, 39
   Agency Management and Infrastructure, 46
   Flaws and Alternatives, 47

3 STRENGTHENING THE SYSTEM 50
   Key Objectives, 53
   Features of Peer Review, 58
   People: Roles of Reviewers, Applicants, Staff, and Practitioners, 67
   Conclusion, 76

REFERENCES 78

APPENDIXES
A Workshop Agenda 81
B Biographical Sketches of Committee Members and
   Workshop Speakers 84

Executive Summary

Peer review is a method used to inform decision making by engaging experts in a critical evaluation of the merits of a product or proposal. It is most commonly known as a mechanism for judging the quality of proposals for research funding, or manuscripts submitted for publication in academic journals.

The focus of this report is on peer review as it is applied to the evaluation of proposals for federal funding of education research projects. The primary source of evidence we use to set forth our conclusions and recommendations about this topic is a workshop we convened in February 2003 in Washington, DC. The agenda for that event, a full transcript of the day's presentations and discussions, and a paper we commissioned to lay the groundwork for our deliberations are all available on the web at http://www7.nationalacademies.org/core/Peer%20Review.html.

A long-standing tool of science policy in the United States, peer review is widely recognized as the preferred method for judging the merits of proposals for research funding. Across the federal government, it is used in a variety of contexts and for a variety of purposes—both scientific and political in nature. It is at once a tool with which scientific judgment is formalized and decisions about the allocation of scarce public resources are legitimized.

In the many federal agencies that support education research,[1] peer review practices vary widely. Historically, this variation has largely been a function of differences in culture, tradition, mission, and the fields and disciplines each agency supports. These factors are important inputs to the development of peer review systems, and each agency should have the flexibility to create a system tailored to meet its needs and to accommodate its circumstances. While we acknowledge this variation and encourage agency flexibility, all peer review systems can and should uphold basic principles of fairness and merit.

For federal agencies that support education research, we recommend that in addition to these considerations, peer review should be explicitly designed, managed, and evaluated to promote two key objectives: to identify and support high-quality scientific research in education and to promote the professional development of the field. Adopting these objectives as guideposts will enable agencies to think strategically about the merits of, and trade-offs associated with, particular practices and design options. To illustrate this central idea, we analyze key elements of peer review through this lens.

IDENTIFYING AND SUPPORTING HIGH-QUALITY RESEARCH

Peer review can foster the development of a high-quality research portfolio in federal agencies that support education research. Two central issues form the core of how to develop a system that supports this goal: deciding who counts as a peer and defining and consistently implementing standards of what high-quality means.

Assembling the group of reviewers is the very crux of the matter: the peer review process, no matter how well designed, is only as effective as the people involved. Judging the competence of peers—individually and as a group—in any research field is a complex task requiring assessment on a

---

[1]The agencies who made presentations at our workshop included the Institute of Education Sciences and the Office of Special Education Programs of the U.S. Department of Education; the Center for Scientific Review and the National Institute on Drug Abuse of the National Institutes of Health; the Education and Human Resources Directorate and the Social Behavioral and Economic Sciences Directorate of the National Science Foundation; and the Office of Naval Research.

number of levels. In education research, it is particularly complex because the field is so diverse (e.g., with respect to disciplinary training and background, epistemological orientation) and diffuse (e.g., housed in various university departments and research institutions, working on a wide range of education problems and issues).

The types of expertise reviewers should bring to the peer review table to identify high-quality education research include the content areas of the proposed work; the theoretical models, methods, and analytic techniques proposed to address the research questions; and the practice and policy contexts in which the work is situated. No single individual is expected to contribute expertise in all of these areas. Rather, panels must bring combined expertise; thus, expertise in the context of assembling peer reviewers should be viewed in terms of the panel as a whole.

Vetting and publicly disclosing reviewers' potential conflicts of interest and biases is essential to identifying panelists who will fairly judge proposals on their merits. In practice, many top-flight researchers predictably have potential conflicts or biases with respect to particular applicants in a research competition: they may have collaborated on projects, coauthored papers, or mentored or taught the investigator seeking funding. Reviewers must be as free as possible from such potential conflicts of interest, as they cast doubt on their ability to judge the proposals on their merit alone. However, because many of the best reviewers are likely to be linked in some way to the work under consideration, if conflict of interest rules are too strict, the talent pool of reviewers can shrink dramatically. Also, the biases, or preferences, that reviewers bring to their work should be aired and balanced across panelists so that no single paradigm or perspective dominates the panel review. The key is public disclosure of potential conflicts and biases so that others can gauge the significance of any identified conflict and bring up those that might not be identified.

Two broad types of diversity are relevant to assembling high-quality panels and to promoting education research quality through peer review: diversity of scholarly perspectives and diversity of groups traditionally underrepresented in education research. Engaging researchers who approach the topic under consideration from a range of perspectives can enrich peer review deliberations by bringing together a diverse set of expertise around a common set of issues and problems. And explicitly reaching out to traditionally underrepresented populations to participate in peer review fosters an environment in which questions are provoked and issues raised that otherwise might not have surfaced, helping to ground the review in the cultural and social contexts in which the work is proposed to be conducted and promoting the quality of the research over time. Actively pursuing diversity along both of these dimensions in an agency's peer review system has other benefits as well, including lending the process legitimacy and enhancing and extending powerful learning opportunities that take place in peer review deliberations.

There is a final and particularly contentious issue related to diversity and to identifying the peers that review in federal agencies that support education research: how education practitioners and community members should be involved. Because education research is applied and attention to the relevance of the work crucial, it is essential to include practitioners and community members in the work of such agencies. Whether and how they participate on panels, however, is a difficult question. A major concern with the practice of including reviewers without research expertise[2] on panels is that it could lead to inadequate reviews with respect to technical merit criteria, a critical aspect of research proposal review in all agencies. In addition, since the field of education research is in the early stages of developing scientific norms for peer review, this important process could be complicated or slowed by the participation of individuals who do not have a background in research. We do see the potential benefits of including practitioners and community members on panels evaluating education research funding applications for identifying high-quality proposals and contributing to professional development opportunities for researchers, practitioners, and community members alike. Thus, we conclude that this option is one of four possible strategies—including reviewing proposals alongside researchers, reviewing proposals after researchers' reviews, serving on priority setting or policy boards, or participating in retrospective reviews of agency portfolios—that agencies could adopt to actively engage practitioner and community members groups in their work.

To promote high-quality education research that is rigorous and relevant, peer review must rest on consistently applied and well-defined quality standards, and these standards should be made clear to applicants and to reviewers. Although the specific criteria by which applications are assessed

---

[2]We recognize that some practitioners and community members do have research expertise. In these cases, the concerns we outline do not apply. Our focus here is on those practitioners and community members who do not bring this expertise to peer review deliberations.

in the review process can and should vary by agency, it is important that each develop specific scales and anchors for reviewers to apply to each evaluation criterion to promote a fair and reliable process. Furthermore, it is essential that reviewers be trained in how to apply the review criteria prior to their evaluation of proposals, so all reviewers approach the task with a set of common understandings about evaluative criteria.

Peer reviewers provide important input to agency leaders about what research applications should be funded. However, it is most often the case that staff is authorized to make final funding decisions. Thus, internal decision making should also be driven by quality considerations. Simply going down a list of applications that peer reviewers have ranked in terms of quality and funding them until available dollars are depleted, for example, can lower the quality of the portfolio as a whole if the quality of the proposals drops off at place that is above (or below) the point at which funding runs out.

Finally, risk is an important element of a high-quality education research portfolio: if agencies never support new work that strikes off in a new direction, challenges core ideas, or approaches a problem from a novel perspective, the potential for significant progress, or even breakthroughs, will be substantially curtailed. The value of risk-taking and innovation should be reflected in funding decisions. This can be accomplished in a number of ways: by including "innovation" or a related construct in the evaluation criteria for the reviews, by allowing agency decision makers to fund applications "out of order" to support riskier proposals, or by retaining a funding mechanism outside the peer review process that is designed to support highly innovative work.

FURTHER DEVELOPING A PROFESSIONAL CULTURE OF INQUIRY

Peer review in federal agencies is rarely designed with the intent of using the tool to enhance the capacity of the field to support a culture of rigorous inquiry. We view this objective as crucial and recommend that peer review systems be designed to support its attainment explicitly. Practices that can support this goal include the targeted inclusion of panelists from a range of scholarly perspectives and traditionally underrepresented groups in education research (note that this strategy promotes this professional development goal as well as the goal of identifying and supporting high-quality research), the use of standing panels, the consistent provision of comprehensive feedback to applicants, the development of agency staff, and extending opportunities for training and professional development among applicants, reviewers, and staff.

The act of deliberating on the merits of research proposals can be a powerful learning opportunity for everyone involved. To encourage the use of peer review as a tool for raising the capacity of the field as a whole, agencies should expand their pool of reviewers by reaching out to groups traditionally underrepresented in education research. Similarly, finding ways to support the participation of junior scholars in the peer review process can be an effective mechanism for mentoring the next generation of education researchers.

Standing panels in which scholars from a range of disciplines and perspectives meet regularly to review research in a given area can offer a rich setting for integrating knowledge across domains and fostering ongoing learning opportunities for participants. They also offer the kind of stability and institutional knowledge that can facilitate positive outcomes when investigators resubmit an application previously reviewed under their auspices. Standing panels do have their drawbacks, however; they can institutionalize bias and narrow the kinds of expertise that can and should be brought to bear on peer review deliberations. Their use should be designed to offset such weaknesses, through the use of such practices as staggered terms for members.

The professional development of applicants—both successful and unsuccessful—can be enhanced through the provision of consistent, comprehensive feedback on their proposals. In this way, the considerations and perspectives of the range of expertise and experiences represented in the peer review process can be communicated to applicants, enhancing the likelihood that their future work will be strengthened. Similarly, interactions between agency staff and prospective applicants can serve as a communication channel between these two key groups in education research.

Since agency staff are important actors in the education research community generally and in the peer review process specifically, their role requires careful consideration. Authorizing staff to be substantively involved in all aspects of research competitions—from writing requests for proposals to running review panels—can draw on and strengthen their expertise and provide useful continuity throughout the process. However, it can also raise thorny questions about fairness. If the same staff work with potential applicants, select reviewers, and play important roles in final decisions about funding, it can create at least the perception that researchers who know agency staff will have an unfair advantage over their less connected peers. Federal agencies that support education research should balance the provision of professional development opportunities for staff and the effective use of their expertise in the process against the need to ensure fair reviews and a system that is viewed as legitimate among a range of stakeholders.

Finally, agencies can enhance the use of peer review as a tool for expanding the capacity of the field by providing training to those involved in the peer review process and offering professional development opportunities for staff and a range of field researchers. Agencies should share this responsibility for making high-quality training widely available with relevant scientific and professional associations.

AGENCY MANAGEMENT AND INFRASTRUCTURE

Effective organizational practices and strong infrastructures are essential to any well-functioning peer review system, including those supported by federal agencies that fund education research. Organizational excellence should be supported by a focus on evaluation, and agencies should consistently analyze the extent to which their practices support stated goals. In addition, effective management requires planning and organization in advance of a review. Scheduling reviews with appropriate amounts of lead time in federal agencies that support education research has been hampered in the past by unpredictable timing of appropriations and widely fluctuating levels of funding. Internal barriers within agencies that slow down program announcements, make peer review difficult to schedule, and result in complicated or burdensome logistics should be minimized. Similarly, legislative mandates that prescribe the details of peer review systems should be minimized, as they can hinder the development of quality systems and impede progress.

An agency infrastructure built to support peer review systems should include, at a minimum, knowledgeable staff, systems for managing the logistics of peer review, and the strategic use of information technologies to support review and discussion of proposals. In particular, we suggest agencies invest in the development of databases that house detailed information on past and prospective reviewers to facilitate the identification of high-quality peers.

CONCLUSION

Peer review has been held up as a quality standard for the conduct and use of education research. It is clear that understanding the complexities and trade-offs associated with this tool is required for the standard to be applied consistently and well. We offer this brief treatment to encourage its use as a tool for promoting important objectives in the improvement of education research and to provide a framework for research policy makers charged with overseeing peer review systems designed to assess proposals for education research funding. Despite its flaws, peer review is a system worth preserving and improving. It can be a powerful driver for the improvement of education research and the field—provided that those charged with overseeing the processes understand the strengths and weaknesses of various approaches and implement them with clarity of purpose.

1

Setting the Stage

Peer review is a method used to inform decision making by engaging experts in a critical evaluation of the merits of a product or proposal. Although it takes on many forms and serves a variety of purposes, it is most commonly known as a mechanism for judging the quality of proposals for research funding or manuscripts submitted for publication in academic journals.

The focus of this report is on peer review as it is applied to the evaluation of proposals for federal funding of education research projects. To set the proper context for our treatment of this topic, this chapter provides an overview of the nature and use of peer review in U.S. science policy; outlines current policies and initiatives with implications for peer review in federal agencies; highlights the inherent tensions between political and scientific values in federal peer review systems (in education in particular), and describes our sources of evidence for, and approach to, setting forth our conclusions and recommendations.

A TOOL OF U.S. SCIENCE POLICY

Although there is no single definition of peer review across the many federal agencies that employ it (U.S. General Accounting Office, 1999), it is essentially a mechanism by which experts ("peers") provide input to decision makers on the merits of proposals for research dollars. Peer review confers the imprimatur of high-quality to research proposals throughout the federal government—judging quality (and potential quality) and lending credence to the allocation of scarce public resources.

The use of peer review in the United States can be traced back to the 19th century; for example, the Smithsonian Institution created an advisory committee for reviewing and recommending funding proposals in the 1840s (Guston, 2000). Since the 1940s and 1950s, peer review has evolved into a cornerstone of federal science policy, and today it is widely recognized as the preferred method for judging the merits of research proposals (Kostoff, 1994), for the ultimate purpose of improving government decision making. More specifically (Guston, 2000, pp. 4-31):

> Reformers have sought to harness peer review to help produce knowledge on which policy makers can rely, for the ultimate purposes of improving decisions, reducing the occurrence of legal challenges and other procedural obstacles, and achieving other political goals.

As a tool of science policy, peer review is embedded in the American system of government. Since it is used to steer the investment of federal funding in research, peer review is necessarily and appropriately influenced by political values and accountable to elected officials for the fairness of its processes and the success of its outcomes. Accountability to the public suggests, among other things, that the process be transparent and legitimate to a broad range of stakeholders.

As a tool for researchers to decide the merits of new research projects and directions, peer review is also part of the fabric of scientific communities.[1] Scientific judgment is formalized through the peer review process, as groups of researchers familiar with an area of scientific inquiry reflect on the likelihood of proposed ideas to advance what is known in productive ways. As such, peer review is a tool through which researchers develop, sustain, and communicate their professional culture, suggesting the need for a buffer from political influences.

Peer review in federal agencies, then, reflects both the principles of democratic accountability and the principles of scientific merit. In practice, upholding both sets of principles simultaneously can be difficult. The ways in which agencies go about promoting both take on many different forms,

---

[1]Although not our focus, peer review is also a hallmark of research funding decision making in the arts and humanities.

and negotiating the proper roles and boundaries of each is an inescapable and constant task, as the description of the current policy context below makes clear.

POLICY CONTEXT

No single policy sets standards for, or provides oversight of the use of, peer review in the federal government. In fact, peer review is largely a practice shaped by culture and experience. However, there are a host of statutes, regulations, and other policy issuances that influence (or could influence) the structure and use of peer review across a broad swath of agencies, including those that fund education research. Some of these policies invoke peer review as a way to promote particular objectives, including enhancing the technical quality and credibility of information disseminated by federal agencies (e.g., U.S. Office of Management and Budget, 2003, 2004), supporting research that is rigorous and relevant to national problems (e.g., Education Sciences Reform Act of 2002, H.R. 3801), and using scientific advisory panels to inform government decisions of many kinds (and thus is subject to the Federal Advisory Committee Act, P.L. 92-463, Sec. 1, Oct. 1972). In addition, there are policies not about peer review per se that nonetheless have potentially significant implications for its management and use. For example, the President's Management Agenda, a recent directive aimed at managing and investing federal dollars more efficiently, has as-yet unknown implications for federal personnel, including those who oversee the peer review infrastructure in scientific agencies.

In the past few years, federal officials have set forth many of these new initiatives and proposed a range of clarifications and modifications to other elements of this policy apparatus, inviting a spirited debate and illustrating the tensions that arise as peer review serves both political and scientific ends. We provide an overview of a few of them here to characterize the current landscape of which our consideration of peer review of education research proposals is a part, to demonstrate the high stakes associated with the topic, and to illustrate and foreshadow some of the complexities of peer review in a range of fields, disciplines, and applications.

For example, the U.S. Office of Management and Budget (OMB)—the agency in the Executive Office of the President charged with developing and overseeing the implementation of the federal budget—recently issued a bulletin to provide guidance for defining government-wide standards for the peer review of "influential" scientific information and assessment (including social science studies). The intent of the guidance is to improve the quality of the information the government uses to make policy, for example, in developing federal regulations that govern the nation's safety, health, and environmental policies (U.S. Office of Management and Budget, 2003, 2004). Although the purview of the bulletin explicitly excludes the peer review of research proposals (our specific topic), the input of the scientific communities critiquing an early draft of the bulletin raised important questions and issues about the roles and purposes of peer review in general, many of which we address in this report. Later in this chapter, we highlight some of these commonalities as prologue to our consideration of peer review of education research proposals in federal agencies.

Another recent example of policy reforms with implications for peer review stems from the competitive sourcing and consolidation directives contained in the President's Management Agenda, the Federal Activities Inventory Reform Act of 1998, P.L. 105-270, and the OMB Circular Number A-76. Overall, these initiatives are intended to promote efficiency in government operations. Agency implementation of these wide-ranging initiatives features, among other requirements, a multiyear effort to catalogue and to assess whether the functions performed by federal personnel—including those who support the peer review infrastructure in research agencies—are "inherently governmental functions" and whether they could be more efficiently performed by private sources. While the scope of this effort and its implications for federal jobs are still in flux, it is possible that organizations like the National Institutes of Health (NIH) Center for Scientific Review (which oversees the peer review of grant proposals to the agency) could be downsized. Because peer review is so central to NIH and other research agencies, many researchers have expressed concern about the potential negative consequences of this initiative for the peer review infrastructure in the federal government (Kaiser, 2003).

The centrality of peer review for funding decisions in scientific agencies and for the use of scientific information throughout the government is also reflected in recent agency planning documents prepared to comply with the Government Performance and Results Act of 1993, P.L. 103-62. The Department of Interior's most recent strategic plan, for example, states: "The world-wide hallmark of good science is the collegial, cooperative, peer review of study plans and experimental results." Similarly, the U.S. Department of Education's (ED) strategic plan cites the need to "articulate clear standards" for peer review as a strategy for raising the quality of research funded or conducted by the department.

The concerns raised by scientists in response to the OMB peer review bulletin and the competitive sourcing efforts, coupled with the prominence of peer review in strategic planning documents in federal agencies, suggest that there is strong consensus about the important role of peer review among researchers and policy makers alike. But because it sits at the nexus of science and government, peer review is not without its controversies in practice. Recent events in the halls of Congress provide another case in point. During debate on the fiscal year 2004 labor, health and human services, and education appropriations bill, an amendment was introduced to eliminate funding for a handful of projects that had passed through the NIH peer review system because the subject of inquiry—human sexuality—was objectionable to some members. A debate ensued about the appropriate role of Congress vis-à-vis the merit-based peer review process. In the end, the amendment was defeated and the projects maintained funding, but the controversy continues.

Recent federal initiatives in education research and the critical role of peer review in it also illustrate the often controversial negotiations and high-stakes debates that characterize peer review in the federal government, providing further context for our consideration of peer review with respect to education research funding in the federal government. Most notable in this regard are a set of federal education policies aimed at applying "scientifically based research" to improve policy and practice. In many recent reauthorizations of the K-12 education laws that govern the federal role in elementary and secondary education, there is explicit reference to the use of research to inform reform efforts. Such language appears over 100 times in the No Child Left Behind Act of 2001 alone. A component of the detailed definition of scientifically based research in the act—which is essentially the standard that federal grantees must meet in providing evidence to support their program choices—is that it "has been accepted by a peer-reviewed journal or approved by a panel of independent experts through a comparably rigorous, objective, and scientific review" (P.L. 107-110, the No Child Left Behind Act). Similar provisions that include reference to peer review appear in the Education Sciences Reform Act, H.R. 3801, legislation passed in 2002 that replaced the Office of Educational Research and Improvement (OERI) with the Institute of Education Sciences (IES) as the primary research arm of the ED.

In crafting these provisions, members of Congress and their staffs aimed to upgrade the quality of research and to promote its widespread use (see, e.g., Sweet, 2002); here again is a reflection of policy makers' faith in peer review. Among many education researchers, however, the insertion of these provisions into federal law has provoked protests about what they view as an encroachment on their profession to define legislatively (politically) what "counts" as rigorous, scientific education research (Feuer, Towne, and Shavelson, 2002; Erickson and Gutierrez, 2002). Arguably, the profile of education research is at a high point, but so too are the controversies in and around the field of education researchers.

In this environment, IES officials have recently made changes to their peer review system. The leadership of the agency contracted out the management of their peer review system, a responsibility formerly held by agency staff. IES director Grover (Russ) Whitehurst explained this decision at the workshop, saying that it was made to reduce the likelihood of bias or the appearance of bias in the agency's peer review system by separating agency staff who develop research program announcements from the review process. In the current system, IES staff generates lists of potential reviewers. In conjunction with the chair of each review panel, the independent contractor then vets and appoints the reviewers, with Whitehurst approving the final list. Concern was raised by participants at the workshop and elsewhere that this arrangement could result in the exclusion of relevant perspectives from the important considerations that take place at the peer review table.

We do not intend to adjudicate the current or future consequences—positive or negative—that may come of any of the initiatives we highlight in this brief sketch of the policy landscape. In addition to providing context for our consideration of peer review of education research proposals, this snapshot of recent events illustrates the complexities inherent in peer review in general and relevant activities in education research specifically, laying the foundation for our discussion of the use of peer review in federal agencies that support education research.

IMPLICATIONS AND THEMES

Taken together, the conversations that have swirled around this array of activity go to the core issues involved in developing effective peer review systems and the proper role of researchers, elected officials, and other stakeholders in it. Indeed, many of the same issues are raised regardless of the type of review or the scholarly field in which the debate is situated. For example, a November 2003 National Research Council (NRC) workshop convened by the Science, Technology, and Law Program on Peer Review Standards for Regulatory Science and Technical Information convened stakeholders to discuss the initial draft of the OMB peer review bulletin. In offering a conceptual overview of issues in this context, Sheila Jasanoff, a leading expert in science policy and author of the influential 1990 book *The Fifth Branch,* noted that peer review serves a number of different purposes in government and that its processes vary substantially across contexts, citing the "endless diversity" of existing models and insisting on the need for flexibility in agencies to develop systems that meet their needs. John Graham, the OMB official leading the development and implementation of the bulletin, stressed the need to bring top experts to the table, but concerns were raised about who to involve and how to deal with potential conflicts of interest and biases. Donald Kennedy, editor-in-chief of *Science* magazine, discussed the importance of, and complexities involved in, developing a process that is sufficiently transparent and inclusive to promote its legitimacy among a range of stakeholder groups, including practitioners and consumers.

These issues were central to the discussion of education research peer review at our own workshop and are prominent themes in this report. Echoing Jasanoff's observation of the multiple purposes that peer review is asked to fulfill and the variation in models across and within agencies that fund education research, we argue for flexibility for agencies coupled with a clear articulation of the objectives each system is designed to serve. We tackle the tough question of what counts as expertise in the diverse and applied field of education research. Specific issues of whether and how to involve stakeholders in the process and how to identify and deal with potential conflicts of interest and bias among candidates for participating in peer review panels are also addressed, picking up on the issues Graham and members of the scientific community raised about assembling panelists. And finally, a theme that runs throughout the report echoes Kennedy's concern of ensuring a system that is widely viewed as legitimate by the many diverse stakeholders in science, including scientific education research.

SOURCES OF EVIDENCE

This report is one in a series designed to highlight and to promote improvements in the quality of scientific research in education. Our consideration of peer review as one important leverage point for promoting quality is informed by three main sources of evidence: the workshop the committee held on the topic in February 2003, a select review of relevant literature, and our own experience on peer review panels.

We designed the workshop to promote a broad-based discussion of the purposes, models, and results of peer review systems used across a range of federal agencies that support education research in light of the recent changes and issues in the policy landscape we have described. To help frame the event, we commissioned Edward Hackett and Daryl Chubin, authors of the highly influential book *Peerless Science: Peer Review and U.S. Science Policy* (Chubin and Hackett, 1990), to write a paper on the institutional and social contexts of peer review of education research proposals and to present major themes at the start of the workshop. We organized the rest of the workshop sessions to address topics and to feature speakers that provided maximum coverage of issues and representation of viewpoints. Workshop speakers included federal officials from the ED; the NIH; the Office of Naval Research (ONR); and the National Science Foundation (NSF). In addition, speakers included investigators from a range of fields in education research and social science disciplines as well as from epidemiology and nuclear physics.

Over the course of the day and a half long dialogue, this diverse set of experts and policy makers provided their perspectives and experiences and, in limited cases, the results of their research, on such issues as the purposes of reviews, selection and training of reviewers, review criteria and scoring systems, roles of staff and stakeholders in the process, and timelines and other management issues. The agenda for the meeting, a transcript of the presentations and discussion sessions, and the Hackett and Chubin paper can be found at http://www7.nationalacademies.org/core/Peer%20 Review.html. The wide-ranging and probing dialogue that resulted from the paper and the event are the main sources of support for the conclusions and recommendations in this report.

A secondary source of evidence for our conclusions and recommendations is a select review of the published literature on peer review. This empirical research base on peer review of research proposals is surprisingly limited; while there are some important exceptions (several of which we cite in this report, and some of which we individually authored), most publications on the topic are based on theoretical arguments and personal experience. We draw most heavily from a few seminal publications that provide a survey treatment of issues in peer review and that focus on education research specifically, including Chubin and Hackett (1990), the U.S.

General Accounting Office (1999), August and Muraskin (1998), and several publications of the NRC. The NRC reports we consulted related to peer review and science policy include *Peer Review in Environmental Technology Development Programs* (National Research Council, 1999), *Evaluating Federal Research Programs: Research and the Government Performance and Results Act* (Committee on Science, Engineering, and Public Policy, 1999), and *Assessing the Need for Independent Project Reviews in the Department of Energy* (National Research Council, 1998). We also relied on NRC reports related to education research, including *Research and Education Reform: Roles for the Office of Educational Research and Improvement* (National Research Council, 1992) and *Scientific Research in Education* (National Research Council, 2002).

Finally, we draw on our own personal experience serving on panels to supplement the evidence gathered during the workshop and in our limited review of published literature. Our collective experience on panels is substantial, including service for such federal agencies as the IES and its predecessor agencies, several directorates of the NSF, a number of study sections in the NIH, the Veteran's Administration, the Department of Defense, and the Department of Energy; state agencies, such as the Massachusetts Department of Health; participation in panel reviews of research proposals to be funded by other national governments, such as those in the United Kingdom, Canada, Japan, Australia, and Israel; research reviews for philanthropic foundations and professional associations, such as the American Educational Research Association, the Association of Teachers of Preventative Medicine, the March of Dimes, the Spencer Foundation, the Markle Foundation, the Russell Sage Foundation, the Sloan Foundation, the All Kinds of Minds Foundation, and the McDonnell Foundation; and in peer review deliberations across a range of disciplines and fields, including sociology, history, psychology, cognition, epidemiology, statistics, cultural anthropology, nuclear physics, and an array of subfields in education research.

OBJECTIVE AND APPROACH

Our main objective in issuing this report is to inform decision makers charged with developing or maintaining peer review systems for education research proposals in a rapidly changing policy context. To meet this objective, we set a number of parameters to frame how we would approach designing the workshop and developing this report. We articulate these parameters to further orient the remaining discussion.

First, our conclusions and recommendations apply to peer review of education research proposals in any federal agency that funds research relevant to education. Our primary sponsor for the event—the National Educational Research Policy and Priorities Board—was disbanded with the passage of the Education Sciences Reform Act, H.R. 3801, in late 2002. That act created the IES, replacing the OERI and calling for the formation of a new policy board that will work with IES leaders on issues related to peer review in the agency. (As of this writing, the president has nominated several individuals to be members of the board; they now await confirmation by the Senate, as required by law.) In addition to informing this new board's work, we also hope to provide direction for other government agencies that fund education research. Thus, we designed the workshop and wrote this report to apply to the range of federal agencies that use peer review (or will in the future) to aid education research funding decisions—including, but not isolated to, the IES.

Furthermore, although the committee did hear about an evaluation of OERI's peer review process in the 1990s, the workshop and this report are not evaluations of OERI or any other agency's peer review system. Rather, we treated the information we learned about agency systems at our workshop as examples of peer review in practice. We describe aspects of these systems, highlighting their strengths and weaknesses in meeting particular objectives and drawing on the experiences of the agency representatives to ground our deliberations and recommendations in the reality of the current federal policy environment.

Finally, our treatment of peer review in this report focuses only on federal systems designed to handle proposals for education research projects. The use of peers to judge proposals or products is common in other pursuits both inside and outside government. In the ED, for example, peer review has been used to judge state accountability plans for implementing certain provisions in Title I of the No Child Left Behind Act, as well as to provide input on state applications for funding under the discretionary programs authorized by the law (e.g., Reading First). In nonprofit and private institutions with research programs (e.g., foundations), peer review is also frequently used. We expect that much of our discussion of the issues and our recommendations will be relevant to these other uses of peer review, but we have not analyzed their generalizability to other such areas explicitly.

One other part of the education research infrastructure in which peer review plays an important role is in manuscript submissions to journals.

We did not take up this kind of peer review at our workshop in any detail and thus do not treat it in this report; we addressed this issue more directly in a later workshop on journals and their role in advancing knowledge in education (the workshop agenda and transcript from this event can be viewed at http://www7.nationalacademies.org/core/Journal%20Standards.html).

ORGANIZATION OF REPORT

To develop a concise report for policy audiences, we treat a complex topic with over 100 years of history and scholarship thematically and selectively. We organize the remainder of this report into two chapters. Chapter 2 provides an analysis of some of the key features of and debates around the peer review of education research proposals. Building on that discussion, Chapter 3 contains our proposals for strengthening and improving peer review systems used to aid decision making about the federal funding of education research.

2

Analyzing Key Elements

On the surface, setting up an effective peer review system seems straightforward: contact the top experts in the field, have them review a set of proposals and provide their input, and fund research projects according to the advice provided. Experience has shown, however, that enacting this simple concept is complicated. How should expertise be defined, especially in the many areas of education research that are multidisciplinary? What kind of criteria should be used to judge the proposals, and how should they be quantified or summarized? How should the process be structured so it is seen as legitimate by a range of stakeholders? What is the best way to organize and support the group? What is the nature of the relationship between the peers and the agency staff and leadership, who typically make, and are ultimately accountable for, final funding decisions?

These are but a few of the multidimensional questions involved in designing, revamping, or evaluating peer review systems. This chapter provides an overview of some of the major components of peer review systems designed to assess education research proposals in federal agencies. We describe and analyze components of peer review processes with respect to how they promote particular objectives. We chose to consider aspects of peer review from this perspective not only because it serves as an effective organizational framework, but also because in our view research policy makers ought to approach their own systems in a similar manner. We conclude with an examination of management issues that influence the extent to which such systems can produce desired results.

From our analysis, we draw six major conclusions:

1. Peer review serves a number of worthwhile purposes. For peer review systems for federally funded education research, two objectives important in their design are the identification and support of high-quality research and the further development of a culture of rigorous inquiry in the field.
2. Federal agencies that fund education research use a range of models for peer review that serve different purposes and objectives.
3. Developing peer review systems involves balancing multiple, and sometimes conflicting, values and thus often requires making trade-offs.
4. Peer review in the federal government is a tool by which agency goals are accomplished and therefore can only be developed, evaluated, and understood as framed by these objectives.
5. Although peer review is not perfect, it is the best available mechanism for identifying and supporting high-quality research.
6. Peer review of education research proposals in federal agencies could be improved in a number of ways.

MULTIPLE PURPOSES AND VALUES

In Chapter 1, we described the nature of peer review in federal government as one that serves both scientific and political ends.

In their paper (see http://www7.nationalacademies.org/core/Hackett Chubin_peer_review_paper.pdf) and presentation to the committee, Hackett and Chubin elaborate the many functions that peer review is called on to serve. At the most basic level, peer review is a mechanism for evaluating the merits of proposals for research funding, thereby influencing the distribution of federal research funds. But it also serves several additional and related functions.

For example, a major reason scientists participate in peer review—a time-consuming task in addition to existing professional obligations—is to have an impact on the field beyond their own investigations. Thus, peer review shapes the accumulation of knowledge over time by recommending a subset of proposed research for implementation. This idea was prominent in workshop discussions. Both Hilda Borko, education professor at University of Colorado and president of the American Educational Research Association, and Penelope Peterson, dean, school of education and social policy and Eleanor R. Baldwin Professor of Education at Northwestern University, speaking on behalf of a group of education school deans,[1] articulated peer review as a force that "shape[s] and envisions" the future of a field. Edward Hackett, sociology professor at Arizona State University highlighted the "communication function" of peer review and its role in "prepar[ing] the ground for the acceptance of new ideas." Finbarr Sloane, of the Education and Human Resources (EHR) Directorate of the National Science Foundation (NSF), echoed these ideas, stating that "there is a huge return on investment for serving on a panel. . . . [Reviewers] get a sense . . . for what national questions other people are posing, and responses to those questions." And Edward Redish—a physicist and physics education researcher at the University of Maryland—also pointed to the benefits for researchers who serve on peer review panels, citing the value he has experienced in "see[ing] what people were thinking about in the field."

Delivering feedback to proposers can also signal the field's (often implicit) standards of quality, reinforcing them in a formal context. Redish made this point about the purpose of peer review most directly, arguing that "peer review is not just about finding scientific merit in particular areas. It is about defining it and creating it." This purpose is particularly salient in education, since current standards of evidence often vary by discipline and subfield. Redish's point also underscores the fact that judging the scientific merit of a proposal for research is different from judging the merits of a research product. Research is by its nature an exercise in being alert to, and systematically dealing with, unexpected issues and questions that arise in the course of an investigation. Therefore, the nature and level of specificity of quality criteria are different when considering a description of how an investigator plans to approach the work than when considering the product of a completed investigation.

Peer review can also be used as a tool for building interdisciplinary

---

[1]This group—called the Education Deans' Alliance—was formed in 2000 to share information and to improve the doctoral training of education researchers at their institutions. It includes deans from schools of education at Columbia University, Emory University, Harvard University, Michigan State University, Northwestern University, Stanford University, the University of California at Berkeley, the University of California at Los Angeles, the University of Michigan, and the University of Pennsylvania.

trust among groups of investigators from different research traditions—again, an important endeavor in an area like education, in which multiple fields and disciplines focus on various aspects of teaching, learning, and schooling. Kenneth Dodge, director of the Center for Child and Family Policy at Duke University, described how engaging in peer review helps draw disparate fields together to better reflect and understand the complexities of educational phenomena.

Another function of peer review is its role as a buffer, creating a privileged space for researchers to make judgments largely apart from political considerations (Hackett and Chubin, 2003). While political considerations drive funding levels and can impact statements of priority areas (National Research Council, 2002), peer review is used to remove decisions about the funding of individual projects from the influence of special interests or other political groups and agendas. Thus, the peer review process offers a space for researchers to apply scientific principles, debate and identify promising lines of inquiry, and offer crucial advice to decision makers that draws on their expertise to advance research-based knowledge.

Workshop discussions also highlighted the role of peer review as a tool for professional development—for proposers, reviewers, and agency staff—to promote a professional culture of inquiry and rigor among researchers. This culture includes an ethos steeped in self-reflection and integrity, as well as a commitment to working toward shared standards of practice (Shulman, 1999; National Research Council, 2002; Feuer, Towne, and Shavelson, 2002). Many workshop participants pointed to the broad "educative" function of peer review to mentor an incoming generation of scholars, to train investigators to review the scholarly quality of proposals, to produce higher quality proposals in the future, and to strengthen connections throughout the field of education research.

Although rarely explicit, peer review is often expected to meet these and many other purposes equally well. It is therefore not surprising that the process can come under fire for not serving any one of them fully. Designing peer review systems, improving existing ones, and assessing their effectiveness requires cognizance of these expectations and the implementation of process options accordingly.

In addition to serving multiple purposes, peer review systems are also designed to serve a set of values, like those of the agency and the fields it supports. These values are sometimes in tension, and they always require a careful balancing act in choosing a course of action. For example, peer review is expected to uphold the value of effectiveness—"to recommend projects that would benefit the field and confer some greater social benefit, to offer advice to proposers, to circulate ideas within a community, and more. Peer review is also asked to be efficient, to do all of this at very low cost, with cost measured in terms of dollars spent on reviews (infrastructure, travel, reviewer compensation) and in hours expended by proposal writers and reviewers" (Hackett and Chubin, 2003, p. 15).

Another example of these value tensions is the trade-off between risk and tradition. Hackett and Chubin (2003) argue that this tension in peer review is a reflection of the tension in scientific communities more generally: research is expected to chart new progress, but to do so systematically and within the broad parameters set by existing knowledge and standards of rigor. During her presentation, Peterson argued that peer review systems ought to "create opportunities for risk-taking and innovative education research."

Simultaneously maximizing efficiency and effectiveness and risk and tradition are just a few examples of the many kinds of values to be balanced—explicitly or implicitly—by peer review systems (see Hackett and Chubin, 2003, for a more complete treatment). The multiple purposes and competing values inherent to peer review, coupled with the complex nature of education and education research, are reflected in a high degree of variability in peer review systems among the many agencies that fund education research. Culture, tradition, and the mission of the agency also exert a powerful influence over the nature of peer review practices. Indeed, it is clear that no single model could suit all purposes and all situations and all fields equally well.

Whether a particular practice will work well depends in large part on the specifics of the situation and the purposes the system is intended to serve. To guide our analysis of peer review practices, we first articulate two broad purposes best served by peer review systems in federal agencies that support education research.

KEY OBJECTIVES OF PEER REVIEW FOR EDUCATION RESEARCH

Taking our cue from this discussion of multiple purposes, we conclude that two broad objectives that ought to guide the design of peer review systems in federal agencies: the identification and support of high-quality education research and the professional development of the field.

The first objective of using peer review as a process to achieve quality research has been front and center in federal agencies that have funded education research for some time (although it is a matter of debate how well various agencies have done so in the past). We strongly endorse explicit attention to education research quality as well as redoubled efforts to strengthen peer review systems for this purpose. Rigorous studies of educational phenomena can provide important insights into policy and practice (and have—see National Research Council, 2002, for examples). But poor research is in many ways worse than no research at all, because it is wasteful and promotes flawed models for effective knowledge generation. Quality is of the essence, and having leaders in the field carefully scrutinizing and screening proposed work is one essential way to promote it.

Although what is meant by quality with respect to education research is a matter of some debate in the field, attending to the rigor and relevance of education research is essential to its health. Peer review systems in federal agencies offer a natural place to engage the field in the contested but crucial task of developing and applying high standards for evaluating the merits of proposed research. Strict rules are not advisable given the interdisciplinary nature of education and the prospective nature of research proposals. However, broad standards, consistently applied in peer review settings, are needed to ensure quality.

Moreover, the current enthusiasm for, and debates surrounding, calls for "scientifically based research" in education and references to the use of peer review provide opportunities for a stronger and more consistent focus on peer review as the means to promote research quality. By defining and upholding high standards of quality in the peer review process, researchers can exert a powerful influence on questions of what counts as high-quality research in particular contexts—providing input directly from the scholarly communities with respect to the implementation of policies stemming from the now numerous definitions of quality research that appear in federal education law (e.g., the No Child Left Behind Act of 2001, the Education Sciences Reform Act of 2002, and bills pending to reauthorize the Individuals with Disabilities Education Act of 1997 and parts of the Higher Education Act of 1965, P.L. 89-329). The insulation of peer review from the political process is important for facilitating this goal.

In our view, the second objective that should guide peer review in federal agencies that support education research is to contribute to the further development of a culture of inquiry in the field. Peer review has not historically been designed to promote such professional development in the federal agencies that support education research. We think it deserves far more attention. As the authors of *Scientific Research in Education* (National Research Council, 2002) argue, we think it is a professional responsibility of education researchers to participate in peer review in federal agencies, and the field ought to harness this system to promote the development of the profession.

Federal education research policy makers also have major responsibility for organizing peer review in ways that foster growth among education researchers. If deliberately developed with this objective in mind, peer review systems can serve this purpose among the many players in the education research field. In the context of peer review, they can usefully be categorized as applicants (people who are seeking agency funds to initiate new work), reviewers (people who review the merits of the proposals for new work), and staff (people who work in the research agencies).

All three of these categories of people are members of the research community, operating in the broader public domain. In the ideal, peer review systems foster enriching interactions, and each group serves both a teaching and learning function to their own benefit and that of others. Chubin and Hackett (1990) argue that this dynamic can improve understanding among all members of the community, enhancing the capacity of the field as a whole.

For example, an applicant can communicate to reviewers cutting-edge ideas in an area of study, stimulating thinking among a broader set of researchers on potential new directions for a field or subfield. In much the same way, the feedback that reviewers provide to applicants often signals areas of contention about new ideas or techniques, preparing the ground for broader scrutiny and consideration of where and how to push the knowledge base and its application. Agency staff teach and learn as well: they familiarize reviewers with relevant agency priorities, goals, review criteria, process specifics, and the particular objectives held in a research competition for advancing the field. In the process of managing and participating in the process, the staff often gain a significant breadth of understanding and knowledge in a field by reading proposals and listening to reviewers' dialogue about the status of the field and the quality of the batch of proposals under review across and within panels. In some cases, agency staff are themselves accomplished researchers who are serving in temporary posts in research agencies. Overall, knowledgeable staff sharpen internal thinking about how to shape and run future competitions.

Having described and justified our choice for the two objectives we hold as most salient for shaping peer review of education research proposals, we now analyze several design features of peer review systems described at the workshop with respect to how likely they are to promote them. Other purposes, including those mentioned in this report, may be relevant to promote in particular contexts and at particular points in the evolution of a line of inquiry in education research. Our intent in setting forth these two objectives is to identify explicitly the purposes we see as most relevant for organizing peer review systems in federal agencies, as well as to provide a structure for analyzing various aspects of peer review systems. Since some peer review practices serve more than one purpose, there is some overlap in the discussion of peer review practices and considerations between the two main sections that follow. In some of these cases, we highlight the tensions that arise and the trade-offs that are often required in the attempt of peer review to serve multiple purposes.

IDENTIFYING AND SUPPORTING HIGH-QUALITY RESEARCH

The formal review of education research proposals by professional peers must be designed to identify and support high-quality research. There are many decisions and practices that undergird this critical function, most of which can be categorized into two areas: the people in the process—Who counts as a peer?—and the criteria by which quality is judged—How is research quality defined? Within each, we take up a set of peer review practices described at the workshop that relates to them most directly.

Who Reviews: Identifying Peers

Deciding who counts as a peer is the very crux of the matter: the peer review process, no matter how well designed, is only as good as the people involved. Judging the competence of peers in any research field is a complex task requiring assessment on a number of levels. In education research, it is particularly difficult because the field is so diverse (e.g., with respect to disciplinary training and background, epistemological orientation) and diffuse (e.g., housed in various university departments and research institutions, working on a wide range of education problems and issues). The workshop discussions brought out several related issues and illustrated the difficulties in, and disagreements associated with, assembling the right people for the job.

Unpacking Expertise

What are the required skills, experiences, and knowledge for peer reviewers to perform their duties? Workshop participants answered this question in a number of ways. In their presentation of the main findings from an evaluation of the peer review system at the former Office of Educational Research and Improvement (OERI) during the mid-1990s, Diane August, senior research scientist, Center for Applied Linguistics, and Penelope Peterson reported on an analysis of the fit between the expertise of reviewers and the competitions they reviewed for. Using the standards for peer reviewers that were in place at the time, they focused on the extent to which each reviewer had content, theory, and methodological expertise. They found a number of disconnects, including a relatively low level of fit on the methodological aspects of the research proposals under review (August and Muraskin, 1998).

Expertise is required in three main areas to identify high-quality education research in the review process: the content areas of the proposed work, the methods and analytic techniques proposed to address the research questions, and the practice and policy contexts in which the work is situated.

At one level, it is self-evident that reviewers need to know something about content to review education research proposals. But "education" is a term covering a vast territory of potential areas of study. Some competitions for research dollars are cast quite broadly (e.g., early childhood development), while others carve out a well-defined subtopic (e.g., effectiveness of pre-K curriculum on school readiness). Content expertise, then, is defined by the research priorities in the competition itself. Even in relatively circumscribed competitions, a wide range of content knowledge is typically required to adequately judge the merits of a set of proposals. Furthermore, the knowledge of content as it applies to teaching and learning that content is important. Referencing Shulman (1986), Borko made this point at the workshop, asserting that in order "to review proposals about mathematics teaching and learning, [reviewers] really do need to know about mathematics, and . . . teaching and learning. Pedagogical content knowledge is kind of the nexus of those aspects of knowledge."

Another dimension of expertise necessary for peer review of education research proposals is knowledge of relevant methodological and analytic techniques. Like any profession, familiarity and facility with the tools of the trade are an essential part of the job. Reviewers must posses a solid grounding in methodological approaches best suited for studying the particular problems or topics reflected in the competition. Competent peer review of the quality of research must be conducted by groups of researchers who are together familiar with both general standards (like those outlined in *Scientific Research in Education*, National Research Council, 2002) and specific standards (relative to particular subfields) and who practice these standards in their own research studies (National Research Council, 1992; Chubin and Hackett, 1990; Cole, 1979).

Finally, reviewers must be grounded in the overarching practice and policy contexts associated with the area under consideration. This foundation is necessary to place the potential contribution of new work in the context of current issues and problems facing education policy makers and practitioners, as well as to consider the kinds of expertise that might be required to carry out the work effectively.

Do all reviewers need to have each kind of expertise to participate effectively? Most workshop participants agreed that not only was it nearly impossible to find people with such breadth and depth of experience and expertise, but also that it wasn't necessary. Rather, we agree with most participants that it is the combined expertise of the group that matters. That is, constructing panels with appropriate expertise requires ensuring that the group as a whole reflects appropriate coverage. Hackett made this point most directly, arguing that it is the "distributed" expertise on a peer review panel that is relevant.

Beyond these three broad areas of competence that we view as essential for peer review panels, additional kinds of expertise relevant to the process surfaced in workshop discussions. For example, Robert Sternberg, director of the Yale Center for the Psychology of Abilities, Competencies and Expertise and the president of the American Psychological Association, suggested that creativity is an undervalued yet critical talent for assessing research quality.[2]

Teresa Levitin, director, Office of Extramural Affairs, speaking from her experience running panels at the National Institute on Drug Abuse at the National Institutes of Health (NIH), referred to a number of personal qualities that make for effective reviewers. Such people listen respectfully and are intellectually open to genres of research outside their realm of expertise. They neither dominate nor acquiesce during face-to-face delib-

---

[2] Due to illness, Sternberg did not attend the workshop but sent his presentation slides for the committee's consideration.

erations about proposals under review. Although we deem these traits as secondary to the three dimensions of expertise we describe here, they are some of the intangibles that influence the success of the peer review process in a very real way and therefore must be considered in vetting reviewer candidates.

Conflicts of Interest and Bias

For peer review to be an effective tool for identifying and supporting high-quality research, it must be credible. Essential to the integrity and legitimacy of the process is ensuring that reviewers do not have a vested interest in the outcomes of the competition that could introduce criteria other than quality into the process. Thus, it is essential to vet potential reviewers for whether they would have a conflict of interest that would prevent them from fairly judging a proposal or set of proposals. At one level, it is the responsibility of agency staff to probe these potential problems. But it is also a critical part of an ethical code of conduct among investigators to be forthcoming about their relationships to the proposed work. As Levitin put it: "the integrity of the system really depends on the integrity of the individual reviewers."

Conflicts of interest may arise in situations in which there is a possibility, or a perceived possibility, that a reviewer, or his or her associates, might gain from a decision about funding. Agencies deal with these issues in different ways. Steve Breckler, of the Social Behavioral and Economic Sciences directorate at the NSF, referenced a "complex array of conflict of interest rules" that applies to peer review of research proposals submitted to the NSF. Brent Stanfield, deputy director, NIH's Center for Scientific Review, mentioned that applicants for funding from the NIH are encouraged to identify "competitors" who they feel would be too influenced by the outcome of the review to serve as fair reviewers, and that panelists with potential conflicts of interest on a particular proposal would recuse themselves from the discussion of its merits. Louis Danielson, director of the Research to Practice Division, Office of Special Education Programs (OSEP), described the interpretation of these and related rules by the U.S. Department of Education that preclude the participation of reviewers with particular affiliations.

A related but distinct idea that shapes the vetting of panelists is bias. Biases are preferences that may influence the degree to which proposals are judged fairly. Everyone has preferences, and researchers are no exception:

their own work and participation in a field frames the way they view the world. The danger comes when these preferences preclude a careful and open-minded reading of approaches that diverge from a reviewer's personal viewpoint.

As important as it may seem to identify and eliminate conflicts of interest and biases in the peer review process, enhancing the likelihood that the system identifies and supports high-quality research renders the pursuit of these absolute goals unattainable and unadvisable. In making decisions about who to include on panels, many top-flight investigators predictably have potential conflicts or biases: they are likely to be very familiar with each other, and they may have collaborated on projects, critiqued each other's work, coauthored papers, or mentored or taught an applicant. At a minimum, they are likely to have already formed views on each other's work. These biases reflect the preferences that investigators have for certain theoretical and methodological practices and their ideas of what the cutting edge in a field is or should be and therefore affect the ways in which proposals are viewed from the outset.

The existence of these relationships and viewpoints raises questions about the impartiality of reviewers to judge the merits of a proposal fairly that must be addressed in vetting investigators for participation on panels. However, if a decision rule regarding conflicts of interest is applied too stringently, the pool of competent reviewers will dwindle significantly. Making conflicts of interest public is essential, but eliminating them altogether is not feasible. And while conflicts of interest should be minimized, it is often the case that agency personnel need the flexibility to exercise their judgment about how to carefully balance the imperative of involving top experts in the process while guarding against reviews that are based on judgments outside the merits of the proposals themselves.

With respect to bias, however, the issue for assembling panels is to achieve a balance of perspectives and biases. The goal is not to minimize biases—as they are inherent in every reviewer—but rather to ensure that no single paradigm or perspective dominates the review panel. As we argue in the section that follows, engaging a range of perspectives sharpens thinking about, and opens avenues for considering, quality in the research that is funded. And as we discuss in the section on quality, so long as reviewers can agree on basic standards of quality, these divergent preferences can be accommodated in the peer review process and indeed can strengthen its outcomes. Without this common framework, however, there is no basis for negotiating differences in productive ways.

Diversity

Two broad types of diversity are relevant to assembling high-quality panels and to promoting education research quality through peer review: diversity of disciplinary and methodological perspectives and diversity of groups traditionally underrepresented in education research. Actively pursuing diversity along both of these dimensions in an agency's peer review system can serve a number of important functions, including lending the process legitimacy, enhancing and extending learning opportunities in peer review deliberations, and promoting the identification and support of high-quality research. We take up the first two of these functions in later sections of the report, focusing on the discussion of quality in this section.

Engaging peers with a range of scholarly perspectives is important for assessing quality in any field, including education research. Redish, drawing on his experience in physics research as well as in physics education research, cautioned on the dangers of peer review systems having a narrowing effect on a field too quickly. He argued that peer review systems ought to reflect an ethos of scientific "pluralism," especially in a field like education research that is multidisciplinary and still emerging as an area of scientific inquiry.

Assembling diverse panels with respect to groups traditionally underrepresented in education research—like racial and ethnic minorities—is also an important consideration that surfaced a number of times in workshop discussions and is especially relevant to education research, as it often grapples explicitly with issues involving diversity. One important aspect of research quality across many of the agencies discussed at the workshop is the relevance or significance to educational problems of the proposed work. Assembling panels with a range of personal backgrounds and experiences can foster an environment in which questions are provoked and issues raised that otherwise might not have surfaced, and help ground the review in the cultural and social contexts in which the work is proposed to be conducted and expected to have an impact.

Vinetta Jones, dean of the Howard University School of Education, made this point directly in posing questions to Grover (Russ) Whitehurst about the diversity of peer review panels at the Institute of Education Sciences (IES). She argued that pursuing excellence in, and specifically ensuring the relevance of, education research projects and programs requires an inclusive approach to the composition of panel membership with respect to racial and ethnic diversity, gender, and other background characteristics.

Whitehurst responded by relaying his personal experience reviewing the publication record of potential peer reviewers, noting that their racial and ethnic background was rarely evident. He agreed that it was essential to ensure that deep knowledge of the populations and contexts in which education research would be conducted is represented in peer review deliberations, but that he seeks to ensure that peer reviewers have this knowledge by reviewing the focus of their previous publications.

These differing viewpoints and strategies underscore the complexities associated with the relationship between quality and group membership on peer review panels. While expertise and the personal background characteristics and experiences of panelists are different constructs, they are often related, at least at this point in history. For this reason, in the long run, we think it is likely that socially and culturally diverse peer review panels will result in a more expansive set of perspectives on the assessment of relevance and significance, thereby improving the overall quality of the research over time. Since quality in the peer review of education research proposals includes both technical and relevance criteria, ensuring a diverse set of panelists who collectively bring the expertise and experience necessary to judge both well should always be the goal.

Practitioners and Community Members as Peers

Should practitioners—for example, state school officers, superintendents, principals, teachers, curriculum developers—be peer reviewers? This is a hotly contested question in many domains of research, one that also pertains to the diversity in perspectives in peer review panels. Various countries and institutions have approached this question in different ways. For example, the Dutch Technology Foundation includes "lay citizens" in their reviews (Hackett and Chubin, 2003). Other institutions have devised innovative ways to involve community members in their work outside the peer review process itself. For example, Harold Varmus, former NIH director, tried to bridge gaps between researchers and community members by setting up a Director's Council of Public Representatives. The council brings together representatives from various groups with an interest in medical research, such as patients and their families, health care professionals, and patient advocacy groups, to advise and make recommendations to NIH on issues and concerns that are important to the broad development of NIH programmatic and research priorities. If one aspect of the quality of education research—as we have argued—is its connection and relevance to policy and practice, then it would stand to reason that those closest to the practice of education ought to bring their expertise directly to the task.

Following this logic, the former OERI and the EHR Directorate at NSF have historically tapped the expertise of practitioners and other stakeholders (e.g., parents) by including them as peers alongside researchers in reviewing the merits of education research proposals. Many workshop participants, however, questioned the implementation of this strategy, and the experience of several committee members led them to raise concerns during the event as well. For example, in their evaluation of peer review panels in the former OERI described at the workshop, August and Muraskin (1998) found that while most of the reviewers in their sample had conducted research in education, a sizable minority had not. In his remarks, Dodge warned that asking individuals without research expertise to evaluate scientific quality "discredits the process." And Hackett, while arguing that peer review in education is a natural place to help bridge policy and practice, acknowledged that practitioner (those without research expertise) participation on review panels could undermine attempts to develop a strong sense of professional culture in the field. It may also serve to introduce political criteria into the review of merit if, for example, advocates participate on panels.

As Hackett suggested, however, there are also benefits associated with engaging the viewpoints of practitioners and stakeholders in peer review panels. Practitioners and stakeholders are typically well qualified to discuss the relevance of a particular proposal and its potential contributions to practice. They may also have comments about the application of an intervention proposed for evaluation. Although they are less likely to have expertise on specific technical aspects of the proposal, such as the design, statistics, and sampling plan, they may provide insights about relevant feasibility concerns.

Moreover, in one of the few studies of the impact of research consumers and advocates on peer review panels, Andejeski et al. (2002) reported that both researchers and consumers found it highly valuable to include consumers (in this case, survivors of breast cancer) on peer review panels for the Department of Defense research program on breast cancer. However, in contrast to the way in which practitioners and stakeholders have often been incorporated into education research panels, the ratio of scientists to lay reviewers was high (averaging about 7:1), consumers were trained on the criteria and the process, and they were assigned specifically to review the applications for the importance and applicability of the research and issues related to human volunteers, such as the burden on the participant. The consumers made their comments after the scientists' review.

Overall, workshop participants and the committee agreed that the participation of practitioners in the education research and review process was critical; whether and how agencies involved practitioners in peer review panels to accomplish that goal varied considerably across and within agencies. For example, NIH has a two-tiered model. First, study sections (most often convened by the Center for Scientific Review), consisting of scientific expert reviewers, judge the scientific merit of proposals. The result of the review is a score and a written summary of the evaluation. Second, institute-specific advisory councils, composed of both scientists and other stakeholders, consider the relevance of the proposals, and in view of both the scientific merit and the potential impact, make recommendations about which proposals should receive funding.

Still another way to systematically engage practitioners in reviewing research is through an approach used by OSEP, whose agency assembles peer review panels of stakeholders to retrospectively assess the value of the agency's portfolio of research in addressing practical ends. This structure, when coupled with peer review by researchers, captures the expertise of both but does not involve practitioners in judging the merits of research proposals directly.

Finally, several agencies include practitioners on priority-setting oversight boards. While separate from the peer review process itself, the identification of areas ripe for research shapes the content of the research competitions and the proposals received in response, indirectly but significantly influencing the policy and practical grounding of the research. For example, the former National Educational Research Policy and Priorities Board and the new National Board for Education Sciences are both modeled on this idea.

How Quality Is Judged

Evaluation criteria—how potential research quality is operationalized for the purpose of peer review—focus the review on specific dimensions of quality. The criteria used to judge research proposals vary across agencies and sometimes across competitions within agencies. All include some assessment of technical quality or scientific excellence ("intellectual merit," "quality of design," "approach") and typically its relevance ("significance," "broader impacts"). Agencies commonly weigh and quantify these criteria to ensure that no proposal would get a high total rating if it scored low on either. As Breckler put it at the workshop, technical merit is necessary but not sufficient; similarly, relevance is necessary but not sufficient. Some agencies also consider the quality of the personnel and management plan (e.g., for larger projects like research centers that include multiple investigators and institutions). Other systems include an overall judgment of quality as well. For example, Danielson, in describing the peer review process at OSEP, said that reviewers score proposals on a 100-point scale, but they are also asked to give an additional recommendation of "approved, disapproved, or conditionally approved." Similarly, the NIH study section assessments include "approval" or "disapproval" as well as overall judgments of quality (e.g., "outstanding," "excellent," etc.).

In most agencies, peer reviewers are asked to assess each proposal against these criteria, to assign corresponding scores as appropriate, and to provide written comments to support their scores and describe strengths and weaknesses in each proposal. Peers discuss their views and scores as a group, and the opportunity to change scores based on group discussion is extended. Once final scores are assigned, staff averages the scores, creates a slate of proposals ranked from highest average score to lowest, and forwards the slate to the head of the agency for final sign-off and funding decisions.

Ensuring quality along the dimensions used by an agency suggests the need to create measures that are both reliable and valid. Reliability in this context refers to the extent to which a research proposal would receive the same ratings, funding outcome, and feedback across multiple independent review panels. Ensuring high reliability is important because it helps to quell fears that the ratings are an anomaly or just a function of the particular group assessing them. Even if ratings are perfectly reliable, however, they may not reflect the intended evaluation criteria—that is, they may not be valid. Reliability does not ensure validity, but without reliability, results and feedback will be inconsistent and almost surely not valid.

At the workshop, Domenic Cicchetti, statistician and methodologist at Yale University and author of seminal publications on the topic of reliability in peer review, provided an overview of his work on reliability in the evaluation of both journal submissions and grant proposals, based on an annotated presentation he prepared for the workshop (Cicchetti, 2003). Analyzing agreement statistics across individual judges involved in peer review of manuscripts submitted to journals for publication, he concluded that reliability was generally low.

How to think about and promote reliability in any form of peer review is a topic of considerable controversy and commentary (see, e.g., extensive commentary on Cicchetti's foundational work in this area in an issue of *Behavioral and Brain Sciences*, 1991). In our view, examining agreement among individual judges is reasonably appropriate for assessing reliability in journal submissions, because reviews are typically conducted independently by mail and then simply averaged. For our purposes in considering research proposal reviews, however, the review process more typically involves group discussion among panelists with different types of expertise and is designed to promote consensus. Since the process necessarily involves interaction and argument, the individual ratings among panelists are not independent. In fact, a panel with diverse content and methodological expertise will be likely to produce a more complete review even though initial ratings by individual panel members may vary widely (that is, be inconsistent with one another). To the extent that the consensus-building processes are effective, analyses of initial independent ratings may underestimate the reliability of group results—that is, they may be poor indicators of the reliability of the group consensus on quality as reflected by group expertise. However, the reliability of panels as a whole, while a more useful construct, is difficult to measure because agencies overseeing reviews of research proposals never have the luxury of convening multiple panels to review the same proposals and then comparing the results across the independent panels.

Validity, as applied to the results of peer review, refers to the extent to which inferences made from the resulting ratings and specific feedback are warranted given the information provided in proposals for research funding (Messick, 1989). It is possible for results to be reliable (consistently repeatable) but still not support valid judgments of the merits and deficiencies of a proposal. In general, validity is considerably more difficult to assess than reliability, and there have been very few studies of the validity of peer review results.

Evidence for validity will vary across the different priorities and evaluation criteria established by different agencies. NSF programs, for example, use two separate criteria: intellectual merit and broader impacts. Measures of validity for intellectual merit ratings might include the extent to which ratings reflect how well relevant theoretical constructs are characterized in a proposal, or the appropriateness of applying a particular statistical test for analyzing the data that will be collected. Assessing the validity of impact ratings might involve examining whether they predict the actual participation of traditionally underrepresented groups in funded projects to a useful extent. Few agencies have the time or resources to invest in true validity studies. The difficulty of establishing the validity of peer review results empirically is, in fact, the major reason why the use of expert judgment is the single best option for proposal evaluation.

Finally, there is an element of quality considerations in peer review that relates to risk. Some agencies incorporate the idea of originality or innovation into the criteria used to assess quality. Indeed, in a recent study, Guetzkow, Lamont, and Mallard (2004) found that multidisciplinary social science peer review panelists often viewed originality as what distinguished worthy from less worthy academic work. Although this idea was not explored in much depth at the workshop, it is an important consideration. Risk can be thought of as a dimension of quality with respect to the broad education research portfolio in an agency. If agencies never support new work that strikes off in a new direction, develops new methods or analytic tools, challenges core ideas, or approaches a problem from a novel perspective, the potential for significant progress, or even breakthroughs, will be substantially curtailed. However, peer review tends to reward proposals that rely on established assumptions, models, and techniques. Risk-taking, therefore, may have to be supported through other funding mechanisms, but so long as it is undertaken to strategically invest in highly innovative work, it can be an important element of federal education research portfolios.

Workshop discussions about research quality analyzed both short-term and long-term aspects of quality, and many participants argued that peer review systems ought to be designed to attend to both. Peer review is typically designed to identify high-quality proposals for a given agency competition. But quality can also be viewed as a long-term prospect. Both Redish and Borko explicitly isolated the potential for peer review to upgrade the future quality of research. Indeed, it could well be that none of the proposals submitted in a particular competition will lead to research of the highest quality. In this case, the only way to improve the quality of education research is to get authors to improve the quality of their proposals. Even when research is funded, feedback on issues requiring additional attention can provide constructive suggestions on how to upgrade future submissions.

FURTHER DEVELOPING A PROFESSIONAL CULTURE OF INQUIRY

Peer review of education research proposals also ought to be designed to support the development of the field of education research. In this section, we analyze facets of peer review that relate most directly to upholding this objective: diversity of perspectives and backgrounds, standing panels, feedback, the role of staff, and training.

Diversity

Several workshop participants suggested that since peer review can and should serve an educative function, efforts to involve a diversity of research perspectives as well as the participation of people from traditionally underrepresented populations in the process were imperative. In response to a question about how agencies ensure diverse perspectives on peer review panels, Steven Breckler told the group that NSF program officers spend a significant amount of time trying to identify people and places that "ordinarily are not plugged into the NSF review process." He also pointed to the NSF criteria for reviewing research applications, which require an assessment of the extent to which the proposed activity will broaden the participation of such groups in the evaluation of the proposals themselves "broader impacts." According to Stanfield, NIH also pays close attention to these issues, relying on a number of mechanisms to promote broader participation, including the use of discretionary funding to support research among underrepresented groups and institutions.

In terms of this professional development goal, workshop discussions also focused on the role of peer review for developing junior scholars, another way to view diversity in the composition of panels. At the workshop, Peterson argued that a critical function of peer review in education research was to promote learning opportunities and growth among early career researchers. Borko made a similar argument, suggesting that peer review be used to "mentor the next generation of researchers." Agency representatives offered examples of how this goal is pursued in practice. For example, Sloane noted that in his work, "we make an effort to have about 20 to 25 percent of our panels be people who are not tenured."

Standing Panels

Panelists can be assembled once to review a single set of proposals (ad hoc panel) or on a regular basis to meet over a predetermined length of time and consider a particular area of research (standing panel). There are strengths and weaknesses of both approaches. Ad hoc panels may be prudent when efficiency must be maximized; the review of small, exploratory grants may also be best served by assembling one-time groups.

To promote professional development and capacity building in the field, standing panels are a very attractive mechanism. Since education researchers come from so many fields and orientations, panels focused on particular issues or problems in education can promote a collective expertise that builds interdisciplinary bridges and facilitates the integration of knowledge across domains. Hackett, drawing from his own experience participating on NSF peer review panels, asserted that establishing interdisciplinary trust is difficult when panels are ad hoc. In contrast, he argued that standing panels that convene groups of investigators regularly around issues or problems can be quite promising in this regard. Standing panels provide a context for researchers to build relationships with scholars they might not otherwise know. Panel members can carry these experiences into their own work and that of their colleagues, forging broader disciplinary connections among more and more researchers studying common phenomena and questions but approaching them from different perspectives.

The use of standing panels is also likely to encourage the participation of top-flight investigators, as these longer term experiences are more attractive as professional learning opportunities than short-term panels. Offering this benefit is particularly needed in education. In their evaluation of OERI, Diane August and Lana Muraskin reported that many former panelists do not view peer review as worthwhile for their career development and trajectory (August and Muraskin, 1998). Although there are surely many factors that lead to this sentiment, it is worth noting that peer review panels at OERI were always ad hoc.

Standing panels can also provide the kind of stability and institutional knowledge that can facilitate positive outcomes in resubmitted proposals. Not all agencies have standard resubmission policies—that is, formal procedures that unsuccessful proposers can follow to respond to the reviews of the proposal and potentially receive funding at a future date. Such processes can identify promising projects in need of further development for funding and provide concrete direction for improvements in specific areas. When an (improved) application is resubmitted, the panel members know the history of its development and can more knowledgably evaluate it on how well the proposers have responded to specific critiques rendered during its initial review.

In addition, when groups of scholars meet regularly in peer review, they provide continuity of vision to programs of research—lines of inquiry in particular areas that together point to new insights, raise new questions, and suggest future directions for agency competitions. Over time, panelists acquire an understanding of the roles and relationships between the field and the agency, enhancing mutual understanding and reinforcing the norms of the culture in the context of the agency's operations. It is the continuity that standing panels bring to an agency's peer review system that is the basis for fostering powerful learning among proposers, reviewers, and staff.

Although well-suited as a professional development tool, standing panels have their drawbacks. Retaining the same people over time can have a narrowing effect on the advice given to agency leadership, which is why many standing panels have term limits. Standing groups develop a consensus view of the field and its needs, which can result in neglecting potentially important lines of inquiry, methodological approaches, or contextual factors. Worse, they can institutionalize the biases the members bring to the work. The potential for these negative consequences is heightened if the members are not explicitly and carefully selected to represent a range of perspectives, if they do not approach their work with a willingness to listen and to consider differences of opinion and approach thoughtfully, and if their biases are not declared, considered, and balanced.

Feedback

Most peer review systems are designed in one way or another to provide substantive feedback to proposers (or would-be proposers) on the strengths and weaknesses of their plans. The mode of feedback can take any number of forms. At the Office of Naval Research (ONR), for example, program officers spend substantial amounts of time working directly with investigators before they write a formal proposal for funding consideration. At many other agencies (e.g., NIH, NSF, and OSEP), the primary feedback mechanism is the provision of written products from the proposal review process—forms completed by reviewers that detail strengths and weaknesses for each evaluation criteria.

Substantive feedback—as well as clear guidelines for resubmission of rejected proposals—can play a vital role in promoting peer review's educative function. At the workshop we learned that a major finding of the OERI evaluation by August and Muraskin (1998) was that the written reviews of proposals were cursory and often merely descriptive summaries of the content of the proposals themselves (rather than analysis of the content with respect to the review criteria). Both Borko and Peterson emphasized the value of feedback in the process and the need to upgrade its use in current systems. At the same time, agency staff from OSEP cited persistent problems getting reviewers to fully document their comments and to clearly justify their ratings, and August and Muraskin (1998) noted this problem in their evaluation of the former OERI's peer review system as well. If peer review is to serve a professional development function effectively, agency staff and reviewers should take these responsibilities seriously and invest the time to fulfill them.

Yet another issue aired at the workshop showed how difficult establishing high-quality feedback can be. Both representatives from NIH described difficulties the agency encountered in recent years because investigators bristled at what they perceived to be inappropriate directives from reviewers. In response, then-director Harold Varmus determined that summary statements emanating from reviews should evaluate the proposed research according to established review criteria, but they should not be tutorials telling investigators how to do their research. In this context, there was considerable discussion about the appropriate level of detail that ought to be part of reviews: How do reviewers and staff balance the need to justify ratings and to communicate effectively with applicants while respecting the professional judgment of applicants? Danielson also raised the issue of resource constraints in this context, suggesting that if the agency were to provide detailed feedback on each of the roughly 4,500 applications they receive each year, they would have to contract the work out due to limited staff resources. We support erring on the side of more detailed information and critique, as this documentation is a key component of a feedback loop that can lead to future improvements in a field.

In addition to reviewers' written feedback, agency staff can also interact with members of the research community—at professional association meetings, workshops convened specifically for principal investigators and future principal investigators, and other such venues—to orient investigators to the agency's priorities and processes. The level of detail, approach, and other such particulars associated with the content and format of proposals is not the same across or even within federal research agencies, and the more familiar proposers and reviewers are with these important process mechanisms, the better the review and, most importantly, the better the products of the review. Explicit training on the nature of feedback should also be provided to reviewers; we take up such training issues in a later section.

Role of Staff

Another key feature of peer review systems is the role of staff in the process. Agency staff are part of the human resources of the research field, playing both teaching and learning roles. There are very real trade-offs associated with the various models of staff involvement in practice today. Three of the agencies represented at the workshop—NIH, NSF, and ONR—nicely illustrate two models at opposite extremes and a hybrid approach to staff involvement. At NIH, the system is very deliberately built to erect a clear separation (sometimes called a firewall) between the staff who write the grant announcements soliciting proposals and developing scientific programs and the staff who select and interact with peers in the review of proposals received in response to those solicitations. In contrast, at ONR, a single staff person (sometimes called a strong manager) performs all of these functions. The system at NSF falls somewhere in between—endowing program officers with a fair degree of authority to shape competitions and to select peers, while creating checks and balances in the system to guard against improprieties.

The benefit of the ONR approach is in continuity of expertise. Knowledgeable staff can follow the process from beginning to end, substantively interacting with members of the field in ways that facilitate learning on both sides and result in work with tight alignment to agency goals. As Susan Chipman, director, Cognitive Science Program, of the ONR, described the process, "ONR staff are the peers—they review proposals and make recommendations for funding." Program officers at ONR often use multiple internal peers to judge research proposals, including potential consumers of the work, since ONR's work is very applied and mission-oriented. Program managers like Chipman actively develop research programs based on the needs of their agency.

The trade-off is that this kind of participation across all parts of the peer review process can result in a loss of external legitimacy. Whitehurst, in describing his plans for peer review at the IES, articulated this downside. In the former OERI, program officers who developed solicitations also selected the peers to review proposals. He acknowledged that this continuity is beneficial because that person becomes expert in all aspects of the competition. The problem, as he described it, is that having responsibility for both kinds of tasks raises the possibility of infusing bias into the system, thereby weakening its overall legitimacy. As he put it, investigators might reasonably wonder: Is everyone getting a fair shake, or are those researchers who are chummy with the program officer getting an unfair advantage? The NIH model, with its built-in firewall, creates a clear boundary and, as Dodge put it, this "keeps it pure."

Describing the NSF process as it relates to these two models, Breckler argued that their hybrid approach taps the best of both worlds by relying on external panels of experts while allowing program officers substantive involvement. He asserted that the tenets of social psychology suggest that the best way to get people to act responsibly is to make them identifiable and responsible for what they are doing, supporting the kinds of roles that staff are authorized to serve: crafting program announcements, selecting peers for review, and settling on a slate to pass on for funding decisions. This approach, he suggested, allows one person to go against the group tendency to be conservative—that is, to reject innovative ideas. And a high level of responsibility helps to attract high-quality officers to the agency.

Responding to questions about the potential abuses of such a system, Breckler argued that the system is rarely compromised because the process is open. The agency mandates extensive documentation of peer review panels, requiring program officers to certify that they have completed parts of the process to the best of their ability and in concordance with relevant policy. To address charges that some investigators may not get the fair shake to which Whitehurst referred, Breckler pointed to a complex array of conflict of interest rules for program officers. Furthermore, NSF has a long-standing tradition of instituting a final check in the process by engaging a committee of visitors to periodically and comprehensively assess research programs on a host of dimensions, including whether such conflict of interest rules were followed. The researchers who are called on to serve this function are asked to carefully scrutinize all aspects of the process to assess its fairness and legitimacy, and the results of the assessment are made publicly available.

Training

For peer review to fulfill a professional development function, explicit training for reviewers, proposers, and staff must be part of the process. But workshop participants revealed that in-depth training is the rare exception rather than the rule in practice.

Training reviewers was raised repeatedly at the workshop as an important element of the peer review process, and agency participants discussed strategies and identified impediments to facilitating successful training. Stanfield described ways NIH helps to familiarize reviewers with the peer review process, including brokering meetings prior to the panel discussion and setting its tone by beginning with experienced reviewers. Breckler asserted that providing model reviews to reviewers would be a helpful strategy, lamenting that this practice is not permitted at NSF. Chipman agreed, suggesting that the use of model reviews could help strengthen a tradition of high-quality reviews in peer review settings for education research.

In describing some training techniques she has used for reviewers at the National Institute on Drug Abuse at NIH, Levitin highlighted several potentially helpful strategies. She suggested that training starts well before the first meeting of the group, is both formal and informal, and is grounded in "general principles and policies." Levitin suggested that if reviewers are well versed in a "few fundamental" ideas, they will be able to provide a fair review. She made clear that there cannot be hard and fast rules for every circumstance, given the very complex nature of review, different types of applications, and other factors, but that there are policies and procedures to guide review in making fair judgments. One key area of training she described relates to teaching reviewers how to apply the review criteria. At NIH, ratings range from 1 to 5, with 1 being the most meritorious. Levitin also stressed that it is important to communicate to reviewers how to provide balanced and thorough reviews, so that the strengths and weaknesses of every application are described and only the stated review criteria are used to assess them.

Training potential applicants was also an area discussed at the workshop. The agencies represented at the workshop relied on a range of largely informal strategies to promote better proposals—such as program officers talking with junior scholars about the grant-writing process—and the degree to which this issue was addressed varied quite a bit. Procedures for resubmission at NIH was the most formal procedure described: with clear and comprehensive written feedback on the weaknesses of a submission, proposers get insights into how to improve their future proposals to the agency and are informed of specific guidelines for resubmitting a revised application in a future grant cycle. Milton Hakel, an industrial and organizational psychologist from Bowling Green State University, suggested that the ability to write rejoinders to reviews could also be instructive. In many respects, the opportunity to revise an application in response to peer review provides this type of opportunity. One-time submission policies without explicit requirements for identifying a proposal as a resubmission and explaining how the grant has been revised misses valuable opportunities for professional development of the researchers.

Finally, the training of staff is similarly important, but no one at the workshop mentioned any kind of professional development for staff involved in peer review systems. Indeed, in their recommendations, August and Muraskin (1998) suggested staff training as a strategy for improving the peer review process at OERI. How to develop training for agency staff would depend on the specific tasks the staff are expected to perform and the skills and knowledge needed to accomplish them effectively.

AGENCY MANAGEMENT AND INFRASTRUCTURE

Like any system, the peer review process must be effectively managed. Negative experiences of many reviewers of education research proposals—especially in the competitions studied in the evaluation of the former OERI by August and Muraskin (1998) and in testimony about peer review at OSEP to the President's Commission on Excellence in Special Education (2002)—in large part derived from poor logistics. Active, careful attention to logistical arrangements enables a smooth peer review process that encourages participation and improves its outcomes. For example, lead time is critical to engaging top scholars in the process. Last-minute planning (often deriving from either legislative or executive branch delays) invariably leads to conflicts with previous commitments, seriously reducing the likelihood of tapping top talent to participate. It also leaves little time for substantive reflection on proposals, leading to cursory and incomplete feedback and, in extreme cases, poor advice to decision makers about funding priorities. Infrequent and inconsistent announcements can set off a "now or never" mentality among researchers, ensuring a high rate of rejection given scarce resources and depleting the pool of potential reviewers. Active proposal management—through triage processes that involve an initial cut through the proposals and assignment of only promising projects to reviewers—can minimize workloads, focusing attention on high-priority areas and making participation manageable for reviewers.

Despite the many anecdotes of how important peer review is to the field and to individual research careers, agency representatives consistently pointed to increasing difficulties in recruiting reviewers. Stanfield identified the logistical hurdles involved with convening face to face meetings as particularly problematic: "It is very difficult to get very busy scientists to come to Washington three times a year for four years." Similarly, Breckler stated, "it is difficult to get people who are going to dedicate themselves to do peer review" and "it is getting increasingly difficult." Incentives for scholars to serve as peer reviewers derive from a number of sources and compel individuals to behave in a variety of ways. Many of the sources are outside the control of any given federal agency (e.g., whether or not service on peer review panels is recognized in promotion and tenure decisions). Agencies can do their part to enable the recruitment of top-flight investigators to review by ensuring that their systems are managed effectively and reviewer workloads are minimized to the extent possible. For example, the August and Muraskin (1998) evaluation reported that many reviewers at the former OERI spent far longer reviewing than the estimated time commitment they had been provided by agency staff.

FLAWS AND ALTERNATIVES

To this point, we have not taken on what might be considered the threshold question: What are the drawbacks to peer review as a mechanism for informing resource allocation of federal research dollars, and are there viable alternatives? There are indeed problems with peer review, some of them significant (see Finn, 2002; Horrobin, 2001; McCutchen, 1997). And there are other ways that research dollars have been and are distributed.

The workshop discussions did not address these questions in any detail. Hackett and Chubin's paper (2003), however, does provide an overview of some of these issues. To set the stage for the committee's recommendations in Chapter 3, and drawing on Hackett and Chubin's analysis, we acknowledge and describe some of the most worrisome weaknesses of peer review. We also identify some of the alternatives they describe for allocating federal education research dollars, ultimately concluding that, despite its flaws, peer review is nonetheless the best available mechanism for allocating scarce education research dollars.

A persistent complaint about the peer review process is the possibility of cronyism—that is, that engaging peers predisposes outcomes to benefit friends or colleagues with no or little regard for the actual merit of a given proposal (Kostoff, 1994). This situation can lead to a kind of protectionism that repeatedly rewards an elite few, narrowing the breadth of perspectives and ideas that is so critical to scientific progress and stunting potentially promising lines of inquiry.

The peer review process can also inhibit innovation. Arguably, peer review is expected to draw the line "between sound innovation and reckless speculation." As Hackett and Chubin (2003, p. 17) argue, "a review system at one extreme could reward novelty, risk-taking, originality, and bold excursions in a field . . . [or] it could sustain the research trajectory established by the body of accepted knowledge by imposing skeptical restraint on new ideas." The closer to the latter pole a system becomes, the more easily it could reject promising ideas as implausible. Current practice is often criticized for being too conservative—a well-known example recounted by Hakel at the workshop is that when the original manuscript describing the double-helix structure of DNA was submitted for publication, it was subjected to peer review and rejected.

What about other ways to allocate research dollars? As Hackett and Chubin (2003) report, Congress has the prerogative to allocate funds through direct appropriation (also termed "earmarking" or "pork barrelling"). In fiscal year 2002, Congress earmarked $1.8 billion for projects at colleges and universities. While not all of this money is for research, earmarks for academia are a useful indicator of the exercise of direct appropriation. And while compared with the roughly $100 billion federal investment in research and development, $1.8 billion is a relatively small amount, it seems somewhat larger in comparison to the $25 billion federal budgets for basic research (all data from analysis by the American Association for the Advancement of Science of the R&D budget; http://www.aaas.org/spp/rd/guihist.htm).

The main deficiency of earmarking is that it circumvents technical expertise, jettisoning altogether the principle that scientific quality ought to be the primary basis for the allocation of research dollars. It also has a corrosive effect on the development of the research profession: without a clear link between rewards (continued funding) and performance (quality of proposals for future work), the core values of science would be eroded significantly (Hackett and Chubin, 2003).

Another alternative is to rely on a single, so-called strong manager who makes decisions on behalf of the agency according to his or her best judgment (as is done in ONR). As Hackett and Chubin (2003, p. 5) observe, "In effect, this is peer review with one peer, so this steward had better be on a par (intellectually and in stature within the field) with those applying for support . . . [and] should understand the field and its needs (which should be clear and widely shared) to ensure that decisions and allocations are wise, legitimate, and effective."

The arguments offered to support the strong manager arrangement include that it is flexible and responsive, and an efficient way to distribute relatively small pots of money. It may also be appealing because the manager is held accountable for performance outcomes (e.g., research-based products that benefit the Navy). However, it would be nearly impossible to scale this approach up to the size of NIH (about $27 billion in fiscal year 2003), and it would face similar difficulties in mid-sized research agencies. More importantly, such concentrated power limits the breadth and depth of expertise that can be brought to bear on proposals and invites serious questions of bias and partiality.

Hackett and Chubin (2003) discuss a third funding alternative—using a formula to allocate resources. Funds may be allocated to states or universities or institutes, then suballocated to groups or individuals according to a variety of additional criteria. Or formulas may be devised based on the past performance of individual scientists, with funds awarded accordingly. Some measure of current need or potential payoff may factor into the equation, as well as the number of researchers at a university or residents in a state. Fair and effective formulas would be hard to devise, and the relative merits of various options endlessly debated.

None of these options for allocating research dollars is perfect, including peer review. When peer review is compared with these alternatives, however, it emerges as the mechanism best suited to promote merit-based decisions about research quality and to enhance the development of the field. This statement does not preclude some type of blended approach in making decisions about what research to fund, however. Indeed, maintaining a variety of funding mechanisms can be leveraged to obviate the weaknesses of peer review. And there are additional design features that can be used in peer review to minimize potential problems. For example, the role of a peer review panel should always be to rank proposals, not to recommend particular decisions about what should be funded, as empowering panelists with making direct recommendations can more easily lead to questions about cronyism and conflict of interest. Term limits, blended expertise on panels, and attention to systematic evaluation of peer review processes and outcomes are additional examples of the kind we address in Chapter 3 that can and should be used to counterbalance the flaws of peer review systems.

In short, peer review as a system for vetting education research proposals in federal agencies is worth preserving and improving. So the question for us is how to strengthen it—a topic we address in the next chapter.

3

Strengthening the System

Our guiding principle in setting forth the recommendations that follow derives from our dual conclusions—detailed in the previous chapter—that peer review of education research proposals ought to focus explicitly on identifying and supporting the highest quality research and strengthening the field to foster a culture of rigorous inquiry.

Peer review in research agencies sets a foundation for developing and sustaining a culture of inquiry and rigor—both within the walls of the agency and in the fields it supports. More so than any single process or practice, creating and nurturing this culture in a research agency is consistently emphasized in reports on peer review in education as well as a range of other fields (National Research Council, 1998, 1999b, 2002; President's Commission on Excellence in Special Education, 2002). Developing this shared sense of commitment to best practice in an agency provides a healthy environment for peer review to function effectively. Specific practices in the peer review systems can sustain the broader culture in the field through reinforcing these norms among applicants, staff, and reviewers, who together are key members of the research field.

In our recommendations, we focus exclusively on the government side of the peer review partnership. We chose this perspective on the basis of an assessment of the current policy landscape and the near-term needs of two key parts of the federal government that support education research: the Institute of Education Sciences (IES) and the Office of Special Education Programs (OSEP). The president has nominated members for appointment to the National Board for Education Sciences of the IES, which, pending confirmation by the Senate, will work with the director to maintain a high-quality peer review system for the agency. And the pending reauthorization for OSEP will almost certainly require changes in its peer review process. Thus, we have attempted to provide a framework for research policy makers who need to revisit their peer review systems in this short report.

Overall, the recommendations we provide are of two kinds: (1) specific ideas to enact the conclusions we set out in the previous chapter and (2) our suggestions for addressing some of the problems related to such issues as logistics and training that were aired during our workshop. In this context, we reemphasize that the evidence we use to support these ideas is based primarily on workshop discussions, and our recommendations should be interpreted in this light.

A final caveat: although we focus on the government's role, we should clarify that the responsibility for ensuring a well-functioning peer review system does not rest solely within the walls of federal agencies. As our depiction of peer review in this report makes clear, the research communities as well as the broader education community all play a part in the process—and thus all share accountability for its success. Without the support, integrity, and participation of these communities—particularly researchers—it is sure to fail.

The committee makes 10 recommendations:

1. Peer review is the best available method to support education research funding decisions. Thus, we recommend that this mechanism be maintained and strengthened.

2. Agencies that fund education research should explicitly focus on two key objectives for peer review: (a) to identify and support high-quality education research and (b) to promote the professional development of a culture of rigor among applicants, reviewers, and agency staff in the education research communities.

3. Agencies that fund education research should develop clear statements of the intended outcomes of their peer review systems and establish organizational routines for ongoing, systematic evaluation of the peer review process.

4. Agencies that fund education research should build strong infrastructures to support their peer review processes. This infrastructure should include (a) knowledgeable staff, (b) systems for managing the logistics of

peer review, (c) technologies to support review and discussion of proposals, (d) a clear mechanism for providing feedback, and (e) standing panels when research priorities are relatively stable.

5. Effective peer review systems require planning and organization in advance of a review. In order to schedule, agencies that fund education research need relatively predictable levels and timing of funding. Internal barriers that slow down program announcements or make peer review difficult to schedule should be minimized. To the extent possible, scheduling problems and complicated or burdensome logistics should be eliminated to support the availability and participation of highly qualified reviewers.

6. Agencies that fund education research should uphold basic principles of peer review but retain flexibility in designing peer review systems to meet their individual needs. Agencies should be accountable for upholding these principles and should provide data on how well their process achieves its goals. External mandates that extend beyond these foundations should be minimal, as they can hinder the development and implementation of high-quality peer review systems.

7. The criteria by which reviewers rate proposals should be clearly delineated, and the meaning of different score levels on each scale should be defined and illustrated. Reviewers should be trained in the use of these scales.

8. As a group, peer review panels should have the research experience and expertise to judge the theoretical and technical merits of the proposals they review. In addition, peer review panels should be composed so as to minimize conflicts of interest and balance biases, promote the participation of people from a range of scholarly perspectives and traditionally underrepresented groups, and provide opportunities for professional development.

9. Agencies that fund education research should involve practitioners and community members in their work to ensure the relevance and significance of their portfolio. If practitioners and community members participate on peer review panels, they should focus on the relevance, significance, applicability, and impact of an education research proposal.

10. Agencies that fund education researchand professional associations should create training opportunities that educate scholars in what the peer review process entails and how to be an effective reviewer.

We begin with two general recommendations that follow from our overarching theme that peer review be strengthened by focusing on two objectives.

KEY OBJECTIVES

Recommendation 1: Peer review is the best available method to support education research funding decisions. Thus, we recommend that this mechanism be maintained and strengthened.

A strong peer review system is a hallmark of successful research and development programs across the federal government. Although there are alternatives to the peer review process for allocating research dollars, none has the same potential for identifying high-quality research proposals and promoting the further development of a professional culture of inquiry among education researchers. Each of the most common alternatives—including a strong program manager who makes the determination, allocations based on formulas, and legislative earmarking—inadequately addresses both of these critical goals that peer review can serve. Peer review is the best mechanism to support the kinds of objectives we hold as critical for the future of the field and the use of education research to improve policy and practice in turn.

The effectiveness of peer review depends heavily on the extent to which specific procedures are designed and implemented to support the stated objectives of the system. Thus, following the logic of the previous chapter, we first state the purposes that in our judgment should undergird peer review of education proposals in federal agencies, and then we make a series of suggestions for how various processes can serve them. We then recommend some basic principles for peer review systems and outline key features of an infrastructure that can support its functions. Peer review involves the expenditure of a good deal of resources, and it is important to ensure that this investment (of federal dollars and researchers' time, primarily) is worthwhile for all.

Recommendation 2: Agencies that fund education research should explicitly focus on two key objectives for peer review: (a) to identify and support high-quality education research and (b) to promote the professional development of a culture of rigor among applicants, reviewers, and agency staff in the education research communities.

Peer review practices in federal agencies have historically been designed based on culture and tradition. We recommend that federal agencies that support education research adopt two objectives—identifying and supporting high-quality education research and promoting a shared culture of rigor in the field—as guideposts as they design, revamp, or evaluate their systems.

One main objective of peer review is to ensure that any research that is funded, published, or used to support education policies or practices meets high standards of quality (Chubin and Hackett, 1990; Hackett and Chubin, 2003). This goal has historically been at the center of agency peer review systems, and should continue to be. Upholding this goal requires that agencies work toward achieving clarity on what is meant by research quality in the context of peer review—a formidable task. Although consensus on this question has been and continues to be elusive in education research more generally (Lagemann, 2000), a starting point for these discussions in peer review panels with respect to technical or intellectual merit criteria could be the principles of scientific education research outlined in *Scientific Research in Education* (National Research Council, 2002, pp. 3-5):[1]

- Pose significant questions that can be investigated empirically.
- Link research to relevant theory.
- Use methods that permit direct investigation of the question.
- Provide a coherent and explicit chain of reasoning.
- Replicate and generalize across studies.
- Disclose research to encourage professional scrutiny and critique.

These principles were not designed to be, nor should they be used as, strict standards to which individual research applications are subjected in peer review.[2] Central concepts embedded in the principles can and should

---

[1]We know, for example, that background materials for reviewers of research competitions of the National Science Foundation's Education and Human Resources Directorate have featured that report's principles as guidelines for assessing quality (or, in their terminology, "intellectual merit"). These principles are meant to apply to scientific research; principles for other important modes of inquiry, such as historical and philosophical studies, are similarly required to ensure the quality of these types of scholarly projects and are not entirely dissimilar from these principles.

[2]The committee that authored *Scientific Research in Education* argued: "Although any single scientific study may not fulfill all the principles—for example, an initial study in a line

be applied fruitfully, however; for example, applications should be scrutinized for the explicit positioning of a researchable question in the broader theoretical and empirical line of inquiry within which it is situated. Also, to extend the principle of a logical chain of reasoning in peer review of funding applications, reviewers can assess the degree to which proposals include a discussion of the kinds of data that will be collected to inform the question and of the sorts of alternative explanations for expected outcomes that could arise during the investigation.

More detailed considerations of what constitutes technical quality in particular competitions and research areas will be required. At the level of specifics, standards for high-quality research require that the research design be consistent with up-to-date accepted practice (or its extension or development) for that design. If an ethnographic study of a school is proposed, for example, reviewers should judge whether the amount of time allocated for investigators to spend in the school is adequate and whether the observational system meets accepted standards for reliability.

Assessment of quality should also include consideration of the relevance or significance of the proposed project: Will it build on what is known in productive ways? Will it contribute to a knowledge base that can inform educational improvement? Is it likely to contribute to solving an important problem of educational practice?[3]

Ensuring that high-quality research is funded at the agency also extends to the internal decision making on fund allocation once the slate of applications is generated by extant peer reviewers. Typically the main product of the peer review process is a slate, or list of proposals, which rank-orders the proposals according to how peers rated them on the evaluation criteria. With variations on the theme, it is common practice for authorized agency staff (typically the director of the division or directorate) to go down the list, funding proposals until they reach the cutoff—that is, the point at which available resources are depleted.

---

of inquiry will not have been replicated independently—a strong line of research is likely to do so" (National Research Council, 2002, p. 52). Also, the principles are more directly applicable to research products than research proposals.

[3]These criteria need not exclude basic research related to educational phenomena. Federal agencies that support education research vary in terms of whether and in what ways they support basic research, and the relevance criteria therefore should be developed and defined to reflect agency priorities.

In practice, there are often reasons to deviate from the linear process of funding the top proposals that can be supported with available resources. For example, funding proposals up to the cutoff is often independent of the relative quality differences between ranked proposals—that is, the line may very well be drawn at a point at which differences in scores are just as easily attributable to random errors as to true differences in quality. Or a set of proposals might not meet high standards of quality such that the cutoff is drawn well below where the quality of the proposals drops off. The converse could also be true: the quality of a proposal could be very high (scoring say, 90 on a 100-point scale), but because it may have been (randomly) part of an especially high-caliber batch of proposals (all 95 or above) or competing for an especially limited number of dollars, it does not make the cut.

These circumstances require careful consideration in making final funding decisions. In the case when the quality of proposals drops off above the cutoff, a decision might be made to fund only those that meet quality standards and therefore not to use all available funding. But it is politically dangerous to decline funding for proposals of questionable quality when funds are available—this decision sends a signal to appropriators that the agency cannot support current funding levels, setting themselves up for funding cuts in the next fiscal year. However, as Whitehurst suggested in describing recent decisions on a slate at the IES, the risks of populating the literature with inferior work may be far greater than a short-term dip in the dollars available for annual research spending.

Finally, federal agencies that fund education research should strive to fund some high-risk proposals in their portfolios. When review criteria include explicit reference to innovation or originality, it is important for applicants to describe and to justify the ways in which the proposed work departs from, and could advance understanding in, current knowledge. However, since the peer review process can be conservative with respect to risk, additional attention to innovation is likely to be needed. For example, the use of a funding mechanism designed to invest a proportion of research funding for high-risk, innovative research could be an effective strategy. Agency leadership should also have the flexibility to make funding decisions "out of order" to support a proposal that might not have been rated highly due to its innovative character.

It is important to clarify that taking calculated risks in funding federal education research does not require a retreat from high standards of quality, nor does it justify supporting work that is technically flawed or of questionable significance to education. Creative, innovative research proposals, like any other, should adhere to standards of rigor and relevance. But because the merits of fundamentally novel questions or approaches can be easily dismissed as peers assess the merits of proposed work through the lens of established traditions and paradigms, agencies need to find ways to reward risk-taking in strategically managing and developing their portfolios over time.

A second objective we hold for peer review is to encourage further development of a culture of inquiry among education researchers. This purpose has not been explicitly adopted on a large scale in the federal agencies considered in this report, and it is especially critical given current concern about the capacity of the field of education to conduct scientific research. Implementing this recommendation will take some time and effort. In Chapter 2, we analyzed several facets of peer review that can be leveraged to promote these professional development opportunities, including panel membership, standing panels, and feedback mechanisms. We elaborate on several specific strategies in recommendations 4, 8, and 10.

In terms of this objective of further developing the field, decisions to contract out aspects of the review process to nongovernment sources should be made sparingly. Outsourcing may be an attractive method for managing the agency's workload, but it can also significantly curtail opportunities for the substantive interactions in the peer review process that foster learning and intellectual growth. Ensuring that agency staff have an opportunity to participate in meaningful ways and seeing that the review process is grounded in the agency's priorities and expertise are critically important in the review process. Outsourcing makes their attainment difficult. Although it may be desirable to outsource logistics, these professional development considerations strongly suggest that internal capabilities to support the intellectual tasks associated with review be retained in-house. For a large research operation like that at the National Institutes of Health (NIH), for example, these internal capabilities have served the agency well. For agencies like the IES, where staff capacity is less developed, however, contracting out aspects of peer review may be an effective interim strategy to build a basic infrastructure. As a general matter, recommendations for outsourcing or otherwise diverting the peer review process to external groups should be made based on a careful assessment of needs and goals in each agency; "one size fits all" recommendations should be avoided.

FEATURES OF PEER REVIEW

The next set of recommendations addresses infrastructure, policy, logistics, and specific mechanisms for strengthening peer review in federal agencies that support education research.

Recommendation 3: Agencies that fund education research should develop clear statements of the intended outcomes of their peer review systems and establish organizational routines for ongoing, systematic evaluation of the peer review process.

Articulating the objectives of the agency's peer review system is a point of departure not only for the design of the system but also for its evaluation. There is surprisingly little systematic evaluation of how and the extent to which peer review processes support or hinder the attainment of system objectives in practice, and we think this status quo is unacceptable.

The benefits of evaluation for organizational growth and improvement are well known. Formative evaluation that generates systematic, ongoing data can identify gaps in service, highlight opportunities for growth, and suggest potential reform strategies. Regularly analyzing these data and feeding them into a continuous improvement loop can be a powerful tool for promoting organizational excellence. And summaries of such data can provide stakeholders with information about how well organizations have met their goals. A sustained focus on the outcomes of government activities is also the spirit in which Congress passed the Government Performance and Results Act of 1993, P.L. 103-62, which mandated that all federal agencies develop strategic plans and monitor their performance with respect to how well they meet specific milestones each year as well as more recent initiatives, like the President's Management Agenda. Thus, we recommend that education research agencies establish procedures for the ongoing review of their peer review practices and results and periodically evaluate whether the goals and purposes of peer review are being met.

Carefully developed process and outcome measures that map to agreed-on objectives must guide data collection and analysis. Using the two objectives we recommend to guide peer review systems in federal agencies that support education research, we offer a few examples of potential data collection and analysis efforts.

Evaluating the extent to which the peer review process results in the identification and support of high-quality research could include such strategies as retrospective assessments of research portfolios by researchers and practitioners (see Recommendation 9), periodic review of the quality of work in progress in a sample of funded projects, and monitoring the publications of investigators supported by agency funds in peer-reviewed journals. Examining the links between peer review practices and the professional development of the field can be pursued in a number of ways. The specificity and quality of reviewer comments on each evaluation criteria and the nature and speed with which applicants were furnished with this feedback can be evaluated and unsuccessful applicants interviewed to ascertain how helpful reviews were for improving their subsequent work. Analyzing the characteristics of reviewers along a number of dimensions (e.g., disciplinary background, gender, race/ethnicity) and their reports of the value of the experience for their career and the field in which they work can provide clues as to how well the system is engaging and helping to develop a broad range of scholars. Management practices can be assessed by systematically surveying agency customers—reviewers and investigators submitting proposals (successful and unsuccessful), for example—and by compiling data on the time allowed for review, scheduling practices, and other activities designed to ease the burden on applicants and reviewers.

Furthermore, the use of committees of visitors to assess peer review practices—a common practice at the National Science Foundation (NSF)—can effectively evaluate the legitimacy and fairness of peer review systems. By focusing and publicly reporting on the implementation of procedures designed to guard against abuses that arise from conflicts of interest, bias, and other potential problems, agencies can institute checks on the system and garner useful information about how to improve it. We see this practice as a useful element of a broader evaluation strategy in federal agencies that support education research.

Calling for evaluation of results is easier said than done. Effectively implementing these activities will require an investment of scarce time and money. However, agencies cannot continue to operate without empirical evidence of the effectiveness of their peer review practices for supporting their objectives. Research agencies by their very nature have the capacity for rigorous inquiry and investigation. We think they ought to use it to critically examine their own practices and to set an example for other organizations inside and outside government.

Recommendation 4: Agencies that fund education research should build strong infrastructures to support their peer review processes. This infrastructure should include (a) knowledgeable

staff, (b) systems for managing the logistics of peer review, (c) technologies to support review and discussion of proposals, (d) a clear mechanism for providing feedback, and (e) standing panels when research priority areas are relatively stable.

In all of the current peer review systems described during our workshop, agency staff play important roles in the process. While the specifics vary, common tasks include preparing grant announcements, identifying and recruiting reviewers, developing and managing reviewer training, handling logistics of the review process, summarizing the comments of reviewers, participating in review meetings, communicating with those submitting proposals, and (in fewer cases) using their own judgment in making final funding decisions. These responsibilities require expertise both in logistics and in the substance of the research areas. A strong peer review system depends on having staff with the managerial and substantive expertise to make the system run smoothly and to capitalize on the knowledge that they and scholarly peers bring to the process.

In particular, the role of the program manager—staff charged with writing requests for proposals for a competition and who will oversee the portfolio of work that will result—requires careful consideration. As described in Chapter 2, there are many different models for this role in peer review, ranging from the firewall approach at the NIH (clear division of labor between program and review staff), to the strong manager approach at the Office of Naval Research (the same staff performs program and review tasks), with many hybrid approaches in between. Whatever the role of program managers, the boundaries should be transparent and articulated to all persons involved in the process and the weaknesses of the preferred staff model compensated for elsewhere in the peer review system.

Models with shared roles threaten at least the perception of the integrity of peer review; potential conflicts of interest can arise easily in selecting reviewers and assigning reviewers to proposals and even the perception of conflict of interest and the inevitable concerns about cronyism will raise questions about the integrity of review. Thus, if such approaches are adopted, they will require the development and consistent implementation of checks and balances to ensure fairness (e.g., having program managers organize reviews of programs other than their own). We see the benefits of substantively engaged staff for promoting their professional development and the learning of those who come in contact with a system staffed by knowledgeable personnel. At a minimum, however, program managers should never attempt to influence reviewers' assessment of the theoretical and technical merit of proposals, nor should their own views on merit be provided at a peer review panel meeting.

Logistical support for peer review is critical to its smooth functioning and to the ability to recruit scholars at the leading edge of their fields to participate in the process. For example, in many competitions, the numbers of proposals and reviewers are large. In the absence of established procedures for handling a high volume of proposals, the process can easily become chaotic. Staff must ensure manageable workloads for reviewers. Practices such as prescreening—sorting proposals before review to weed out applications that do not meet minimum standards or to focus review on controversial or borderline proposals—can be helpful in this regard. For example, we support enacting one of the recommendations emanating from the evaluation of the Office of Educational Research and Improvement (OERI) peer review (August and Muraskin, 1998) suggesting that staff eliminate applications for funding activities that do not involve research.

In determining the optimal size of review panels, staff must balance cost and efficiency criteria with the need for multiple perspectives and backgrounds. An ideal size does not exist—these determinations must be made in the context of the particular circumstances of each review. A reasonable minimum number is three: one person obviates the need for peer review altogether, and with two people there is no way to adjudicate highly divergent conclusions. At the other end of the range, when the size of a panel grows larger than 12 or 14, in-depth discussion of individual proposals is inhibited by the short amount of time each panelist can speak as well as abbreviated opportunities for meaningful and inclusive interaction. The overarching consideration is to ensure adequate expertise (see Recommendation 8) while keeping group size manageable. Soliciting additional ad hoc reviews by those who work in the specialized areas of particular competitions can be helpful in infusing needed expertise while maintaining reasonable panel size.

Additional logistical supports could include well-managed databases. To assist staff in recruiting groups of reviewers that cover the breadth and depth of expertise needed in a given competition, agencies can develop electronic banks of outstanding reviewers. These databases can include contact information, areas of expertise, disciplinary affiliation, demographic data, and strengths and weaknesses of previous reviewers (e.g., skilled writer, synthesizer of information, excellent listener). Active maintenance of this tool will be required to ensure its usefulness. Identifying and tracking the pool of reviewers can also be an effective way to ensure the broad participation of people with diverse viewpoints and backgrounds in an agency's peer review process, an issue addressed by Recommendation 8.

Written documentation of processes, timelines, roles and responsibilities, and review criteria as well as face-to-face training in such areas as how to apply review criteria (see Recommendation 7) are also extremely helpful in fostering a positive environment. To the extent possible, schedules with ample lead time for initial reviews and time for group discussion should be established and followed; without sufficient time resources, reviewers cannot carefully study or discuss proposals, and few purposes will be served well. Such circumstances have long-term implications as well, since they will almost surely leave reviewers dissatisfied and less likely to agree to participate in the future.

Enhanced applications of technology can also facilitate peer review and smooth logistics. At NSF, computer systems provide reviewers with quick and easy ways of recording their reviews, access to other reviewers' comments, and support for substantive discussions of proposals. These systems can be used to minimize the time reviewers have to spend on "process" considerations and enhance opportunities for interactions. Technology can also improve communication at a distance, when costs or timing prohibit face-to-face meetings of reviewers. However, we concur with workshop participants who argued that face-to-face meetings both improve the quality of discussion and provide incentives for reviewers to participate in reviews (since they are more likely to gain from such interactions).

It is worth emphasizing the point that the immediate benefits from competent staff, clear and well-executed procedures, and useful technologies all contribute to longer term payoffs in the form of incentives for scholars to serve as peer reviewers. Several workshop participants noted that the motivations for serving as a reviewer are not financial, but rather a desire to serve and influence the field and the opportunities to learn from the discussions. When the process runs smoothly, discussions are engaging, and the impact of the reviews are evident, reviewers will be motivated to continue; when the process seems clumsy, communication thin and hurried, and impact uncertain, reviewers may decline the next invitation.

For peer review systems to meet the overall goals of supporting high-quality research and providing professional development for the field, procedures must be developed to facilitate communication about the proposals, among the group of reviewers and among the reviewers, applicants, and staff. The amount and type of feedback given on proposals varies across the agencies represented at the workshop, in part because of the effort needed and the varying instruction and training given to reviewers. A greater proportion of agency budgets devoted to consistent and thorough feedback from reviewers to applicants through agency staff and written communications, along with better training for reviewers (e.g., giving them model reviews, providing training in the application of the review criteria), would enhance the role that peer review plays in strengthening research. Here again, these dual objectives of peer review in federal agencies that fund education research should always be kept in mind.

A policy that allows unsuccessful applicants to revise and resubmit their proposals based on previous review can be an excellent vehicle for explicitly linking feedback to future (improved) submissions. Such opportunities can help develop a field, allowing opportunities (especially for researchers in early career stages) to hone and refine ideas and to ensure that promising ideas are not lost in the vagaries of the review process. Indeed, education researchers commonly complain about one-time submission processes (President's Commission on Excellence in Special Education, 2002).

Standing panels can be an attractive part of the agency infrastructure as well. If the general areas of research to be supported are stable, standing panels have several advantages: they make it easier to recruit top scholars as reviewers by increasing the prestige for serving and reducing the need for extensive training before each review cycle. Standing panels facilitate development of consistent interpretations of rating criteria. They are especially conducive to the professional development goal of peer review, since panels can set standards that are maintained as reviewers begin and finish their terms, also providing for the professional development of reviewers. The use of standing panels ("study sections") at NIH exemplifies these possibilities. Agencies that rely solely on ad hoc review panels miss valuable opportunities to develop the human resources of education research. We therefore recommend that standing panels be established for review of education research proposals whenever the substantive focus is reasonably stable over time.

Standing panels often require that additional ad hoc reviewers be added when the topics of supported research change substantially across competitions and each new competition requires a different mix of expertise. Furthermore, the extended terms of standing panel members can lead to stagnated or narrow perspectives, so policies such as staggered terms which infuse new people and ideas into the group, are necessary to counterbalance this effect. And because of the length of service and influence of standing panel members, carefully selecting individuals with a range of perspectives and backgrounds is very important.

In this context, the role of ad hoc panels should be clearly conceptualized in the peer review philosophy at the agency. Ad hoc panels are most useful when a new priority is under consideration or when agencies desire to initiate a significant program of research in a particular area. By augmenting with ad hoc panels, the tendency of standing panels to be risk-averse can often be minimized. Ad hoc panels may also be necessary in agencies with relatively small research portfolios, given the cost of conducting peer review, especially if these priorities fluctuate on a year-to-year basis. The latter situation makes a standing panel especially difficult unless the priorities are related and the pooled expertise of the review group is adequate across different priorities.

> **Recommendation 5: Effective peer review systems require planning and organization in advance of a review. In order to schedule, agencies that fund education research need relatively predictable levels and timing of funding. Internal barriers that slow down program announcements or make peer review difficult to schedule should be minimized. To the extent possible, scheduling problems and complicated or burdensome logistics should be eliminated to support the availability and participation of highly qualified reviewers.**

Ensuring a well-managed process, especially providing ample time and organized scheduling, once again invokes the trade-off of costs and efficiency versus the efficacy of peer review in accomplishing its core objectives (see Recommendation 3 for specifics on implications for agency infrastructure).

In education research, there is a long history of uncertainty over appropriation cycles (see, for example, National Research Council, 1992). When funding is uncertain, competitions cannot be established well in advance and creating standing panels can be difficult. This situation not only affects the quality of research proposed (as applicants are forced to produce rushed proposals), but also makes it difficult to recruit reviewers. If schedules cannot be set up in advance, managing peer review effectively is almost impossible. Reviewers are often unavailable due to prior commitments and, if they do agree to serve, insufficient lead time to thoroughly evaluate the proposals can doom a review. These problems are compounded if internal clearances prior to a competition are extensive and time-consuming (President's Commission on Excellence in Special Education, 2002).

When schedules of announcements are not regular, the field cannot plan and develop thoughtful proposals. Unpredictable and infrequent competitions may attract a high proportion of the top scholars in an area. That leaves an impoverished pool from which to select reviewers. For a peer review system to work well, both strong applicants and strong reviewers must be available on a regular basis. Standing panels can help promote regularity in scheduling and training. But such pools should be used to form committees with regular schedules, not just represent a pool from which reviewers can be drawn when an irregular competition is held. Establishing this kind of stability is essential to helping to grow a culture of rigorous inquiry in education and improving the knowledge base in turn.

Again, we encourage the management of workloads through pre-screening. So long as applicants receive written feedback, it is not necessary to exhaustively discuss every proposal at a meeting. The panel needs time to deliberate and should focus on proposals for which there is potentially high merit as well as those for which there may be disagreements among reviewers.

Finally, attracting and maintaining a high-quality pool of reviewers requires smooth logistics. If the meeting requires complicated travel, poor accommodations, or other sources of administrative burden, reviewers will be tired, demoralized, and less inclined to participate in future panels.

Recommendation 6: Agencies that fund education research should uphold basic principles of peer review but retain flexibility in designing peer review systems to meet their individual needs. Agencies should be accountable for upholding these principles and should provide data on how well their process achieves its goals. External mandates that extend beyond these foundations should be minimal, as they can hinder the development and implementation of high-quality peer review systems.

Peer review mechanisms must adhere to basic principles and be accountable for results. Basic principles for peer review include a dedication to ensuring the scientific merit of proposals; independence from political interference with respect to merit; appropriate expertise on panels; straightforward and publicly available procedures for reviews that promote fairness and integrity; and a mechanism for providing feedback to applicants. Overall, agencies should be accountable for instituting a fair process that leads to funding high-quality research that is seen as significant by consumers. Policy makers and consumers should expect to see independent evaluations of the peer review system as well as evaluations of the agency portfolio (see Recommendation 9 for the role of practitioners in ensuring accountability).

Beyond these considerations, agencies need the flexibility to design and manage their peer review systems. Research evolves in unpredictable ways. Peer review systems must be supple enough to respond to emerging needs and opportunities and to guard against a narrowing of the field. Mandating mechanisms for peer review through legislation may rob the agency of the flexibility it needs. In particular, mandates that extend beyond the authority to conduct peer review and outlining the overall structure can impede the capacity of the peer review mechanism to meet its objectives. For example, as the President's Commission on Excellence in Special Education recently noted in its report (2002), legislative requirements about the composition of review panels are especially difficult for an agency and can have deleterious effects on the ability of the peer review system to identify and support high-quality education research.

Recommendation 7: The criteria by which reviewers rate proposals should be clearly delineated, and the meaning of different score levels on each scale should be defined and illustrated. Reviewers should be trained in the use of these scales.

The agencies represented at our workshop all used different evaluation criteria in their peer review processes. The extent to which the criteria were defined, and the nature and intensity of training for reviewers on how to apply those criteria, varied as well. Given differences in mission and other factors, it is reasonable to expect variation in review criteria; however, we recommend that attention be paid to ensuring criteria are clearly defined and based on valid and reliable measures. We also recommend that the development of training materials and implementation of tutorials for reviewers become standard operating procedure.

Agencies should strive to ensure that the evaluation criteria for peer review be clearly defined and based on valid and reliable measures. In our judgment, reliability (and validity) can be improved for the ratings assigned to proposals as well as for the descriptive feedback associated with scores and group discussion.

At the workshop, Domenic Cicchetti concluded that there was potential for significant improvement in the reliability of ratings across reviewers through careful training on the rating scale criteria and on the rating process itself. This finding is consistent with a large literature on job performance ratings (Woehr and Huffcutt, 1994; Zedeck and Cascio, 1982) indicating the importance of careful definition of scale "anchors" and training in the rating process. Training could not only improve the consistency of initial ratings across reviewers on a panel, but also facilitate group discussion that leads to stronger consensus and reliability of group ratings. It can have the added benefit of improving the validity of the feedback provided to applicants by better aligning the feedback with the specific evaluation criteria, both in terms of the particular scores given and the descriptions of strengths and weaknesses. For all of these reasons, we concur that clearly defined measures and effective training for reviewers on the use of the scales are essential.

We point to the benefits of training throughout this report. In the context of review criteria, training is important to ensure that reviewers understand how to approach the evaluation of proposals and how to assign specific ratings to each criterion. At the workshop, Teresa Levitin of the National Institute on Drug Abuse provided several useful ideas for how to illustrate key concepts to reviewers about the review criteria. To our knowledge there are few such models from which to learn about effective training practices in the context of peer review in federal agencies. Our recommendation is that agencies place stronger emphasis on developing, evaluating, and refining traning programs to ensure that reviewers are applying criteria in ways that are intended, contributing to the process in effective ways, and learning from the experience.

PEOPLE: ROLES OF REVIEWERS, APPLICANTS, STAFF, AND PRACTITIONERS

The next set of recommendations address the types of people who should participate in reviews and the kinds of training needed for the education research communities.

Recommendation 8: As a group, peer review panels should have the research experience and expertise to judge the theoretical and technical merits of the proposals they review. In addition, peer review panels should be composed so as to minimize conflicts of interest and balance biases, promote the participation of people from a range of scholarly perspectives and traditionally under-

represented groups, and provide opportunities for professional development.

The first priority for assembling a peer review panel is to ensure that it encompasses the research experience and expertise necessary to evaluate the theoretical and technical aspects of the proposals to be reviewed. For agencies that fund education research, we define "theoretical and technical aspects" to refer to three areas: (1) the substance or topics of the proposals, (2) the research methods proposed, and (3) the educational practice or policy contexts in which the proposal is situated. Relevant experience and expertise should be determined broadly, based on the range of proposal types and program priorities. If, for example, a specialized quantitative research design is being proposed, at least some reviewers should have expertise in this design; if a specialized qualitative research design is proposed, some reviewers should have expertise in this design.

In addition, it is the range of proposal types and program priorities, not their frequency or conventionality that should determine the scope of the panel's experience and expertise. In most cases, individual panelists will have relevant experience and expertise in one or more, but not all, of the topics and techniques under review. Thus, it is the distributed expertise of the review panel as a whole, and not the characteristics of individual members, that establishes the appropriateness of the panel for the task. In this way, peer review is "intended to free [decision making] from the domination of any particular individual's preferences, making it answerable to the peer community as a whole, within the discipline or specialty" (Harnad, 1998, p. 110).

Thus, peer reviewers of research proposals should be chosen first and foremost for their experience and expertise in an area of investigation under review. Ideally, reviewers will not harbor biases against other researchers or forms of research, will not have conflicts of interest that arise from the possibility of gaining or losing professionally or financially from the work under review, and can be counted on to judge research proposals on merit alone. But in practice, researchers in the same field often do know each other's work and may even know each other personally. They may have biases for or against a certain type of research. They may be competitors for the same research dollars or the same important discovery or have other conflicts of interest associated with the research team proposed in a study. In such situations, impartiality is easily compromised and partiality not always acknowledged (Eisenhart, 2002). However, Chubin and Hackett

(1990) argue that increases in specialization and interdisciplinary research have shrunk the pool of qualified reviewers to the point at which only those with a conflict of interest are truly qualified to conduct the review. Potential conflicts of interest and unchecked biases are a serious limitation of peer review. In the long term these limitations can be addressed by expanding the pools of qualified reviewers, through training and outreach to experts traditionally underrepresented in the process.

In assembling peer review panels, attention to the diversity of potential reviewers with respect to disciplinary orientation as well as social background characteristics is important for a number of reasons. Diverse membership promotes the *legitimacy* of the process among a broad range of scholars and stakeholders. If peer review panels are consistently homogenous with respect to discipline, race and ethnicity, or other category, it will send a signal to those who have been excluded from participating that they are not relevant actors in education research, and that their concerns and perspectives are not valued in the work of the agency. Thus, efforts to promote diversity should be part of the public record.

Diversity is also related to *quality*. Peer review panels made up of experts who come from different fields and disciplines and who rely on different methodological tools can together promote a technically strong, relevant research portfolio that builds and extends on that diversity of perspectives. Similarly, diverse panels with respect to salient social characteristics of researchers can be an effective tool for grounding the review in the contexts in which the work is done and for promoting research that is relevant to a broad range of educational issues and student populations.

Finally, actively recruiting panelists from diverse backgrounds to participate in the process can extend professional *opportunity* to a broader pool of researchers, building capacity in the field as a whole. Social characteristics affect the training researchers receive (because of the schools they attend, the topics and designs they are likely to pursue in school, and the jobs they anticipate for themselves) and in turn affect the experiences and expertise they develop (Harding, 1991; Howe, 2004). Thus, explicit attempts to engage traditionally underrepresented groups in the peer review process can improve access and opportunity, resulting in an overall stronger field and more relevant research.

As we have discussed (see Recommendation 2 in particular), peer review can provide a rich context for further developing researchers into the culture of their profession and should be explicitly designed to promote the attainment of this objective. This function of peer review is often underutilized in the push to make funding decisions efficiently. Opportunities for engaging panel members in activities that further their professional development are compromised when panels do not include broad representation of relevant experience and expertise, when panel members do not deliberate together, and when time does not permit differences of perspective and position to be aired and debated. Such opportunities for developing investigators—both experienced and inexperienced with respect to sitting on review panels—to the research ethos are compromised when clear requests for proposals are not available and when good feedback is not provided to proposers. These limitations also reduce the incentive for strong researchers to contribute their time and expertise to peer review: Why should they contribute if so little will come of their efforts and if they will gain so little from the experience?

Attending to promising scholars at early stages of their careers can also target professional development opportunities for up-and-coming researchers who have solid credentials but less experience reviewing. The testaments of many workshop participants citing early experiences serving on NIH (standing) panels as career-changing are indications of the potential of peer review to develop early career researchers. It is important, however, that promoting the participation of rising scholars in the context of peer review be balanced against the need to tap the best intellectual talent for review.

We need to be clear that by supporting peer review as a mechanism for developing researchers we do not mean to suggest inculcating researchers to a culture based on cronyism and traditionalism. To prevent the isolation of perspectives and favoritism for well-established names and institutions from taking hold, checks on the system must be in place. That said, the very foundation of the research process rests on the development of a commitment to scientific norms and values, which can and should be reinforced in the context of peer review (National Research Council, 2002).

Recommendation 9: Agencies that fund education research should involve practitioners and community members in their work to ensure the relevance and significance of their portfolio. If practitioners and community members participate on peer review panels, they should focus on the relevance, significance, applicability, and impact of an education research proposal.

Education research, by its very nature, focuses on issues with high social relevance. As a result, it is important that the process of funding that research in federal agencies includes input from a variety of stakeholders who include, but are not limited to, teachers, principals, superintendents, curriculum developers, chief state school officers, school board members, college faculty, parents, and federal policy makers (for ease of exposition, we refer to these groups collectively as "practitioners and community members" henceforth). These individuals can provide a wider base of expertise from which to examine educational issues and they can also typically provide a wider demographic perspective to inform decision making.

The question, then, is not whether to involve practitioners and community members in the work of federal agencies that support education research, but how. All research agencies have mandates that involve the need to address the societal benefits of proposed research. In education, this often translates as ensuring that the research is relevant to practice and feasible in the context in which it is proposed. To adequately assess research on this criterion, it is incumbent upon the agencies to involve persons beyond the research communities who can help judge the social relevance and benefits of the funded projects in its portfolio. Indeed, the inclusion of practitioners and community members in the work of federal agencies that support education research can be thought of as another dimension of diversity in peer review and funding deliberations.

As we describe in Chapter 2, the variation in agency practice suggests that there are many ways in which practitioners and community members can provide input to the work of federal research agencies. We struggled ourselves to sort out the best place to engage practitioners and community members. Ultimately, we conclude that these agencies should have the flexibility to use one or more of the four mechanisms we describe here to ensure their active participation:

- Panel review of proposals alongside researchers;
- Second-level review of proposals after researchers' reviews;
- Priority-setting or policy boards; and
- Retrospective reviews of agency portfolios.

The first and most controversial practice used in some agencies involves the inclusion of practitioners and community members on peer review panels alongside researchers. Since this approach is a significant topic of interest generally and among the workshop participants specifically, we analyze the underlying issues as they pertain to the review of education research proposals in federal agencies in some detail and outline the conditions under which such an approach could be beneficial to all involved.

A major concern with the practice of including reviewers without research expertise[4] on panels is that it could lead to inadequate reviews with respect to technical merit criteria, a critical aspect of research proposal review in all agencies. In addition, since the field of education research is in the early stages of developing scientific norms for peer review, this important process could be complicated or slowed by the participation of individuals who do not have a background in research.

We also see the potential benefits of including practitioners and community members on panels evaluating education research funding applications to help identify high-quality proposals and to contribute to professional development opportunities for researchers, practitioners, and community members alike. With respect to quality, practitioners and community members are well suited to provide insights about the relevance and significance of research proposals—an important evaluation criterion across all agencies represented at the workshop. As we argue above, evaluating the technical merits of research—another critical evaluation criterion—is best addressed by seasoned researchers. However, there may be feasibility or practical issues associated with particular study design features that practitioners and community members could help identify. In this way, they can contribute to the judgment of technical merit by lending expertise about the likelihood that a design can be successfully implemented in a particular educational setting (although many researchers also have experience with implementation). Because practical and technical issues overlap in this way, if practitioners and community members serve on panels, they should fully participate in all aspects of the review process, including written reports prior to meetings and discussion and ratings processes during panel meetings.

Including practitioners and community members on panels can also enhance their professional development and that of their researcher peers by providing opportunities for these two disparate groups to understand and appreciate each others' perspectives and contributions. Thus, the peer review process would need to be structured to provide opportunity for meaningful interactions among panelists. Through these interactions, practitioners and community members could learn more about education re-

---

[4]We recognize that some practitioners and community members do have research expertise. In these cases, the concerns we outline do not apply. Our focus here is on those practitioners and community members who do not bring this expertise to peer review deliberations.

search and methods and be more enthusiastic about its potential for improving schools. And researchers could learn more about pressing educational issues and the practicalities of researching them, leading to improvements in research design and implementation that better fits district, school, or classroom practices and organizational features.

If, for these or related reasons, practitioners and community members are included on panels, we recommend that the ratio of researchers to practitioners and community members be high and that maintaining manageable panel size be an additional consideration in whether and how to include them in reviews (see discussion of Recommendation 4). In the authorizing statute for the Office of Special Education and Rehabilitative Services, for example, there are many categories of practitioners and community members required to participate on panels. As a practical matter, this could mean that these groups have a disproportionally large impact on evaluating research proposals relative to their research peers or that, in an attempt to ensure adequate research expertise is represented, panel sizes become unwieldy. Neither scenario is ideal.

Furthermore, attention to developing a pool of qualified reviewers (see Recommendation 8) would need to extend to practitioner and community member groups as well—it is critical that *all* reviewers, including those without research expertise, be carefully and rigorously selected to participate and contribute in a positive way. All peer reviewers—whether they are researchers, teacher trainers, dissemination specialists, administrators, parent trainers, policy makers or others—should be deeply knowledgeable about the area under investigation and screened for potential conflicts of interest and biases.

Finally, to engage practitioners and community members on peer review panels successfully, it is critical that agencies provide thorough training to all reviewers so they understand the expertise they are expected to bring to bear to the review and can participate in the process effectively. In the case of practitioners and community members, then, special attention should be focused on their role in evaluating the significance, feasibility, and applicability of the research. We also think that panel chairs will need additional training to succeed in effectively facilitating group processes when disparate groups are represented at the same peer review table.

There are additional promising ways in which practitioners and community members can and should be meaningfully involved in the education research allocation process in federal agencies. Most of the conditions we describe as important to ensure the success of direct practitioner involvement on panels apply to these options as well: no matter what the strategy, fostering opportunities for meaningful interactions, providing training, and developing and vetting candidates are all essential practices.

The NIH model for involving stakeholders is an attractive option. Stakeholders serve on advisory boards that provide a second level of review—after the assessment of technical merit has been made—that evaluates the grants proposed for funding in terms of their significance and relevance for practice. These advisory boards at NIH also help establish priority areas for their respective institutes.

The role of the NIH advisory boards as setting priorities is yet another way that agencies have employed to engage practitioners and community members. For example, the former National Educational Research Policy and Priorities Board and the National Board for Education Sciences were both created to work with agency leadership to guide the development of programmatic priorities for education research, and by statute require the inclusion of both researchers and practitioners and community members. While the role of these board members does not include the review of individual proposals, practitioners and community members who serve on such boards nonetheless can exert a powerful influence over the policies and practices used in peer review and the nature and type of research the agency seeks to fund.

A final way that agencies can ensure active practitioner and community member involvement is one currently used by the U.S. Department of Education's OSEP to comply with the Government Performance and Results Act of 1993, P.L. 103-62. The agency assembles panels of researchers and stakeholders (including parents of children with disabilities and special education teachers, among others) to comprehensively and retrospectively evaluate the investments OSEP has made along two key dimensions: rigor and relevance. In this way, people "on the front line" are engaged in critically assessing the relevance of the research for addressing their needs. We see this process as a good example of tapping expertise appropriately in federal research agencies, which should be investigated further for its applicability to other agencies and settings.

In sum, education research is strengthened by a rigorous review of proposed projects. Practitioners and community members who represent diverse viewpoints bring important perspectives to education research. Their participation in the work of federal agencies that support education research should be ensured in ways that capitalize on their strengths: assessing the relevance and societal significance of the research.

Recommendation 10: Agencies that fund education research and professional associations should create training opportunities that educate scholars in what the peer review process entails and how to be an effective reviewer.

No matter what regulations or procedures are established for the peer review process, the process can only be as good as the individuals involved. Without explicit training, many scholars in education research may be unfamiliar with the peer review process for obtaining agency funding. The particulars of how to develop proposals for various agencies may not be transparent. And if they are asked to act as reviewers, it cannot be assumed that researchers understand their responsibilities or how to conduct themselves on a panel. This situation is particularly acute for investigators who are beginning their careers and have little or no experience as peer reviewers. Thus, to improve the quality of proposals submitted to funding agencies and the reviews of those proposals, training activities must be developed for writing proposals and conducting reviews.

Because researchers write proposals for paper presentations, books, and other activities, it is often assumed that the requirements for writing a proposal for external funding are similar. While most scholarly proposals do contain similar elements—the importance of the research question, how the study is to be conducted, what one expects to find, and what importance it has to the field—proposals for external funding require a particular level of clarity and specificity that is not typical in other areas. It is not just the level of detail that distinguishes proposals for external funding: such proposals also have to be uniquely conceived and written according to guidelines that can change within and across the various agencies that support education research.

Requests for proposals from agencies typically specify the range of questions, the populations that can be studied, designs for studying them, and the funding level to conduct such work. Although there are announcements for most funding opportunities, investigators still may need assistance understanding if their work falls within the call for proposals, or whether designs that are not entirely in scope but are innovative in approach would be acceptable. Much of this uncertainty could be dispelled with regular communication between funding agency personnel and investigators and efforts to make the process transparent to all.

One way to address these issues systematically would be for the professional associations, such as the American Educational Research Association

(AERA), the American Sociological Association, the American Psychological Association, the American Anthropological Association, and others, to hold workshops on how to write proposals to federal agencies. These workshops should involve agency personnel and individuals who have been successful in the proposal process. Examples of outstanding proposals that succeeded in the review process could be distributed and discussed. It would be particularly worthwhile if the agencies identified proposals that were especially well written and resulted in work that made important contributions to the field.

Several organizations already sponsor similar kinds of opportunities (e.g., the Spencer Foundation, AERA, and the National Academy of Education). Access to these and related experiences should continue to be made available to all, with special emphasis (as is currently the case with some existing programs) on engaging researchers in their early career stages and who come from traditionally underrepresented groups.

Roles and responsibilities for peer reviewers will differ across agencies, areas under investigation, the level of development of a field of research, and the resources available for peer review. Regardless of the roles chosen, they must be made clear to reviewers in advance. As we discuss in connection with Recommendation 7, reviewer training on the use of evaluation criteria is a must. Furthermore, reviewers should follow a basic code of conduct, which includes acting professionally, avoiding personal innuendos, listening to others, airing disciplinary and ideological biases, and continually scrutinizing the potential contribution of the study being proposed. Other training needs will vary by agency goals and associated processes.

Based on workshop discussions, we see this as an area in major need of improvement in most agencies. The National Institute on Drug Abuse has a program to train investigators selected for review panels, which was described at the workshop by Teresa Levitin. Although not widely implemented, it could be a prototype for developing materials and training reviewers, especially for reviewers in education and other social science fields. There are likely to be other models in different agencies that use peer review worth examining in this context.

CONCLUSION

Peer review has been held up as a standard for enhancing the quality and utility of education research. Understanding the basic issues associated with this tool is required for the standard to be used effectively. We offer this brief treatment to help education research policy makers approach the task of improving peer review in this era of evidence-based education. It is our view that the current emphasis on peer review is welcome—provided that those charged with overseeing the process understand the strengths and weaknesses of various approaches and implement them with clarity of purpose.

References

Andejeski, Y., Bisceglio, I., Dickerson, K., Johnson, J.E., Robinson, S.I., Smith, H.S., Visco, F.M., and Rich, I.M. (2002). Quantitative impact of including consumers in the scientific review of breast cancer research proposals. *Journal of Women's Health & Gender-Based Medicine, 11*(4), 379-388.

August, D., and Muraskin, L.D. (1998, October). Strengthening the standards: Recommendations for OERI peer review. Summary Report prepared for the National Educational Research Policy and Priorities Board. Washington, DC: U.S. Department of Education.

Chubin, D.E., and Hackett, E.J. (1990). *Peerless science: Peer review and U.S. science policy.* Albany: State University of New York Press.

Cicchetti, D. (1991). The reliability of peer review for manuscript and grant submissions: A cross-disciplinary investigation. *Behavioral and Brain Sciences, 14,* 119-186.

Cicchetti, D. (2003). *The peer review of scientific documents: Suggestions for improvements.* Précis for paper to be presented at the Workshop on Peer Review of Education Research Grant Applications, National Research Council, Washington, DC, February 25-26. Précis can be found at http://www7.nationalacademies.org/Core/PeerRevNatAcadSci-2-26-03.pdf.

Cole, J. (1979). *Fair science: Women in the scientific community.* New York: The Free Press.

Committee on Science, Engineering, and Public Policy. (1999). *Evaluating federal research programs: Research and the Government Performance and Results Act.* Washington, DC: National Academy Press.

Eisenhart, M. (2002). The paradox of peer review: Admitting too much or allowing too little. *Research in Science Education, 32*(2), 241-255.

Erickson, F., and Gutierrez, K. (2002). Culture, rigor, and science in educational research. *Educational Researcher, 31*(8), 21-24.

Feuer, M., Towne, L., and Shavelson, R.J. (2002). Scientific culture and educational research. *Educational Researcher, 31*(8), 4-14.

Finn, C.E., Jr. (2002). The limits of peer review. *Education Week, 21*(34), 30, 34.

Guetzkow, J., Lamont, M., and Mallard, G. (2004). What is originality in the humanities and the social sciences. *American Sociological Review, 69*(2), 190-212.

Guston, D.H. (2000). The expanding role of peer review processes in the United States. Paper presented at the U.S.-European Workshop on Learning from Science and Technology Policy Evaluation, Evangelische Akademie Baden, Bad Herrenalb, Germany, September 11-14.

Hackett, E.J., and Chubin, D.E. (2003). *Peer review for the 21st century: Applications for educational research*. Paper prepared for the Workshop on Peer Review of Education Research Grant Applications, National Research Council, Washington, DC, February 25-26. Paper can be found at http://www7.nationalacademies.org/core/HacketChubin_peer_review_paper.pdf.

Harding, S. (1991). *Whose science? Whose knowledge? Thinking from women's lives*. Ithaca, NY: Cornell University Press.

Harnad, S. (1998). The invisible hand of peer review. *Nature* (November 5).

Horrobin, D.F. (2001). Something rotten at the core of science? *Trends in Pharmacological Sciences, 22*(2), 1-22.

Howe, K. (2004). A critique of experimentalism. *Qualitative Inquiry, 10*(1), 42-61.

Hutchings, P., and Shulman, L.S. (1999). The scholarship of teaching: New elaborations, new developments. *Change, 31*(5), 11-15.

Jasanoff, S. (1990). *The fifth branch: Science advisers as policymakers*. Cambridge, MA: Harvard University Press.

Kaiser, J. (2003). Can outsiders do better in managing NIH grants? *Science, 299*, 1837.

Kostoff, R.N. (1994). Assessing research impact: Federal peer review practices. *Evaluation Review, 18*(1), 31-40.

Lagemann, E.C. (2000). *An elusive science: The troubling history of education research*. Chicago: The University of Chicago Press.

McCutchen, C.W. (1997). Peer review: Treacherous servant, disastrous master. *Technology Review, 94*(7), 28-36, 40.

Messick, S. (1989). *Validity*. In R.L. Linn (Ed.), *Educational Measurement, Third Edition* (pp. 13-104). New York: Macmillan Publishing.

National Research Council. (1992). *Research and education reform: Roles for the Office of Educational Research and Improvement*. Committee on the Federal Role in Education Research. R.C. Atkinson and G.B. Jackson (Eds.). Commission on Behavioral and Social Sciences and Education. Washington, DC: National Academy Press.

National Research Council. (1998). *Assessing the need for independent project reviews in the Department of Energy*. Board on Infrastructure and the Constructed Environment, Commission on Engineering and Technical Systems. Washington, DC: National Academy Press.

National Research Council. (1999). *Peer review in environmental technology development programs*. Committee on the Department of Energy-Office of Science and Technology's Peer Review Program, Board on Radioactive Waste. Washington, DC: National Academy Press.

National Research Council. (2002). *Scientific research in education*. Committee on Scientific Principles for Education Research. R.J. Shavelson and L. Towne (Eds.). Division of Behavioral and Social Sciences and Education. Washington, DC: The National Academies Press.

Natonal Research Council. (2003). *Srategic education research partnership.* Committee on a Strategic Education Reseearch Partnership. M.S. Donovan, A.K. Wigdor, and C.E. Snow (Eds.). Washington, DC: The National Academies Press.

President's Commission on Excellence in Special Education. (2002). *A new era: Revitalizing special education for children and their families.* Washington, DC: U.S. Department of Education.

Shulman, L.S. (1986). Those who understand: Knowledge growth in teaching. *Educational Researcher, 15*(2), 4-14.

Shulman, L.S. (1999). Taking learning seriously. *Change,* July-August, 11-17.

Sweet, R.W., Jr. (2002). *Legislative intent behind scientifically based research imperatives.* Unpublished presentation.

U.S. Congress. (2002). *No Child Left Behind Act of 2001.* Public Law 107-110, Washington, DC: Author.

U.S. Congress. (2002). *Education Sciences Reform Act.* Washington, DC: Author.

U.S. General Accounting Office. (1999). *Peer review practices at federal science agencies vary.* Washington, DC: Author.

U.S. Office of Management and Budget. (2003). Proposed bulletin on peer review and information quality. *Federal Register, 68*(178), 54023-54029. Available: http://www.whitehouse.gov/omb/fedreg/030915.pdf [6/29/04].

U.S. Office of Management and Budget. (2004). *Revised information quality bulletin for peer review.* Washington, DC: Author. Available: http://www.whitehouse. gov/omb/inforeg/peer_review041404.pdf [6/29/04].

Woehr, D.J., and Huffcutt, A.I. (1994). Rater training for performance appraisal: A quantitative review. *Journal of Occupational and Organizational Psychology, 67,* 189-205.

Zedeck, S., and Cascio, W.F. (1982). Performance appraisal decisions as a function of rater training and purpose of the appraisal. *Journal of Applied Psychology, 67,* 752-758.

Appendix A

Workshop Agenda

Peer Review of Education Research Grant Applications:
Implications, Considerations, and Future Directions
February 25-26, 2003

Tuesday, February 25

8:30 a.m. **Welcome and Goals for Workshop**
Lauress Wise, Committee Chair, Committee on Research in Education and President, Human Resources Research Organization (HumRRO)
Lisa Towne, Study Director, Committee on Research in Education, Division of Behavioral and Social Sciences and Education, National Research Council

9:00 a.m. **Historical Context for Grants Peer Review**
Edward Hackett, Professor, Department of Sociology, Arizona State University

10:00 a.m. **Break**

10:15 a.m. **Education Research and Peer Review: A Perspective from the Institute of Education Sciences**
Grover (Russ) Whitehurst, Director, Institute of Education Sciences (IES), U.S. Department of Education

11:00 a.m. **Goals and Purposes of Grants Peer Review: Perspectives from Investigators**

Hilda Borko, University of Colorado, Boulder, and President-Elect, American Educational Research Association

Penelope Peterson, Eleanor R. Baldwin Professor and Dean, School of Education and Social Policy School of Education, Northwestern University

Robert Sternberg, IBM Professor of Psychology and Education and Director, Center for the Psychology of Abilities, Competencies, and Expertise, Yale University and President, American Psychological Assocation

Kenneth Dodge, William McDougall Professor of Public Policy Studies and Professor of Psychology, Duke University

Milton Hakel, Professor and Eminent Scholar, Department of Psychology, Bowling Green State University

Edward Redish, Professor of Physics, University of Maryland, College Park

12:00 p.m. **Lunch**

12:45 p.m. **Perspectives from Investigators, Continued**

1:45 p.m. **Peer Review Models: Perspectives from Funding Agencies**

Finbarr (Barry) Sloane, Program Director, Interagency Education Research Initiative, Directorate for Education and Human Resources, National Science Foundation

Steven Breckler, Program Director for Social Psychology, Directorate for Social, Behavioral, and Economic Sciences, National Science Foundation

Brent Stanfield, Deputy Director, Center for Scientific Review, National Institutes of Health, U.S. Department of Health and Human Services

Susan Chipman, Program Officer, Cognitive Sciences Program, Office of Naval Research

Louis Danielson, Division Director, Research to Practice Division, Office of Special Education Programs, U.S. Department of Education

APPENDIX A 83

3:00 p.m.   Break

3:15 p.m.   Perspectives from Funding Agencies, Continued

4:30 p.m.   Selecting and Training Peers
               Teresa Levitin, Director, Office of Extramural Affairs,
                  National Institute on Drug Abuse, National Institutes of
                  Health, U.S. Department of Health and Human Services
               Brent Stanfield, Deputy Director, Center for Scientific
                  Review, National Institutes of Health, U.S. Department
                  of Health and Human Services

5:30 p.m.   Adjourn

Wednesday, February 26

8:30 a.m.   Report on Strengthening the Standards: An Evaluation
               of OERI Grants Peer Review
               Diane August, Center for Applied Linguistics
               Penelope Peterson, Eleanor R. Baldwin Professor and Dean,
                  School of Education and Social Policy School of
                  Education, Northwestern University

10:00 a.m.   Break

10:15 a.m.   The Reliability of Peer Review for Grant Submissions
               Domenic V. Cicchetti, Senior Research Scientist,
                  Yale University School of Medicine

11:15 a.m.   Wrap-up Discussion
               Members of the Committee on Research in Education
               Audience

12:15 p.m.   Adjourn

Appendix B

Biographical Sketches of Committee Members and Workshop Speakers

COMMITTEE MEMBERS AND STAFF

Lauress L. Wise (*Chair*) is president of the Human Resources Research Organization (HumRRO). His research interests focus on issues related to testing and test use policy. He has served on the National Academy of Education's Panel for the Evaluation of the National Assessment of Educational Progress (NAEP) Trial State Assessment, as co-principal investigator on the National Research Council's (NRC) study to evaluate voluntary national tests, and as a member of the Committee on the Evaluation of National Assessment of Educational Progress (NAEP). He has been active on the NRC's Board on Testing and Assessment, the Committee on Reporting Results for Accommodated Test Takers: Policy and Technical Considerations, and the Committee on the Evaluation of the Voluntary National Tests, Year 2. At HumRRO, he is currently directing an evaluation of California's high school graduation test and a project to provide quality assurance for NAEP. Prior to joining HumRRO, he directed research and development on the Armed Services Vocational Aptitude Battery (ASVAB) for the U.S. Department of Defense. He has a Ph.D. in mathematical psychology from the University of California, Berkeley.

Linda Chinnia is an educator with the Baltimore City Public School System. During a 32-year career, she has served as an early childhood teacher, a senior teacher, a curriculum specialist, an assistant principal, a principal, and the director of elementary school improvement. Currently she serves as an area academic officer, supervising 35 elementary and K-8 schools. She has been an adjunct instructor at the Baltimore City Community College, Coppin State College, Towson University, and Johns Hopkins University. She has taught courses in early childhood education, elementary education, and educational supervision and leadership. She has B.A. and M.A. degrees from Towson University.

Kay Dickersin is a professor at the Brown University School of Medicine. She is also director of the U.S. Cochrane Center, one of 14 centers worldwide participating in The Cochrane Collaboration, which aims to help people make well-informed decisions about health by preparing, maintaining, and promoting the accessibility of systematic reviews of available evidence on the benefits and risks of health care. Her areas of interest include publication bias, women's health, and the development and utilization of methods for the evaluation of medical care and its effectiveness. She was a member of the Institute of Medicine's Committee on Reimbursement of Routine Patient Care Costs for Medicare Patients Enrolled in Clinical Trials, the Committee on Defense Women's Health Research, and the Committee to Review the Department of Defense's Breast Cancer Research Program. She has an M.S. in zoology, specializing in cell biology, from the University of California, Berkeley, and a Ph.D. in epidemiology from Johns Hopkins University's School of Hygiene and Public Health.

Margaret Eisenhart is professor of educational anthropology and research methodology and director of graduate studies in the School of Education, University of Colorado, Boulder. Previously she was a member of the College of Education at Virginia Tech. Her research and publications have focused on two topics: what young people learn about race, gender, and academic content in and around schools; and applications of ethnographic research methods in educational research. She is coauthor of three books as well as numerous articles and chapters. She was a member of the NRC's Committee on Scientific Principles in Education Research. She has a Ph.D. in anthropology from the University of North Carolina at Chapel Hill.

Karen Falkenberg is a lecturer in the Division of Educational Studies at Emory University. She is also the president of the Education Division of Concept Catalysts, a consulting company that has a specialization in science, mathematics, and engineering education reform. She works both nationally and internationally. She was the program manager for the National Science Foundation funded local systemic change initiative in Atlanta called the Elementary Science Education Partners Program, and has been a mentor for SERC@SERVE's Technical Assistance Academy for Mathematics and Science and for the WestEd National Academy for Science and Mathematics Education Leadership. She also served on the National Academy of Engineering's Committee for Technological Literacy. Earlier, she was a high school teacher of science, mathematics, and engineering and was featured as a classroom teacher in case studies of prominent U.S. innovations in science, math, and technology education. Before she became an educator, she worked as a research engineer. She has a Ph.D. from Emory University.

Jack McFarlin Fletcher is a professor in the Department of Pediatrics at the University of Texas-Houston Health Science Center and associate director of the Center for Academic and Reading Skills. For the past 20 years, as a child neuropsychologist, he has conducted research on many aspects of the development of reading, language, and other cognitive skills in children. He has worked extensively on issues related to learning and attention problems, including definition and classification, neurobiological correlates, intervention, and most recently on the development of literacy skills in Spanish-speaking and bilingual children. He chaired the National Institute for Child Health and Human Development (NICHD) Mental Retardation/Developmental Disabilities study section and is a former member of the NICHD Maternal and Child Health study section. He recently served on the President's Commission on Excellence in Special Education and is a member of the NICHD National Advisory Council. He was a member of the NRC's Committee on Scientific Principles in Education Research. He has a Ph.D. in clinical psychology from the University of Florida.

Robert E. Floden is a professor of teacher education, measurement and quantitative methods, and educational policy and is the director of the Institute for Research on Teaching and Learning at Michigan State University. He has written on a range of topics in philosophy, statistics, psychology, program evaluation, research on teaching, and research on teacher education. His current research examines the preparation of mathematics teachers and the development of leaders in mathematics and science education. He has a Ph.D. from Stanford University.

Ernest M. Henley is a professor emeritus of physics at the University of Washington. He has served as the dean of the College of Arts and Sciences at the University of Washington and as director and associate director of its Institute for Nuclear Theory. The focus of his work has been with space-time symmetries, the connection of quark-gluons to nucleons-mesons, and the changes that occur to hadrons when placed in a nuclear medium; at present he is working in the area of cosmology. He was elected to membership in the National Academy of Sciences in 1979 and served as chair of its Physics Section from 1998 to 2001. He is a fellow of the American Academy of Arts and Sciences and served as president of the American Physical Society and as a member of the U.S Liaison Committee for the International Union of Pure and Applied Physics. He has a Ph.D. in physics from the University of California, Berkeley.

Vinetta C. Jones is an educational psychologist and the dean of the School of Education at Howard University. During a 30-year career in public education, she has maintained a singular focus: developing and supporting professionals and creating institutional environments that develop the potential of all students to achieve high levels of academic excellence, especially those who have been traditionally underserved by the public education system. She has written and lectured widely on issues related to the education of diverse populations, especially in the areas of academic tracking, the power of teacher expectations, and the role of mathematics as a critical factor in opening pathways to success for minority and poor students. She served for eight years as executive director of EQUITY 2000 at the College Board, where she led one of the largest and most successful education reform programs in the country. She has served on numerous boards and national committees and was inducted into the Education Hall of Fame by the National Alliance of Black School Educators in 2000. She has a B.A. from the University of Michigan and a Ph.D. in educational psychology from the University of California, Berkeley.

Brian W. Junker is professor of statistics at Carnegie Mellon University. His research interests include the statistical foundations of latent variable models for measurement, as well as applications of latent variable modeling in the design and analysis of standardized tests, small-scale experiments in psychology and psychiatry, and large-scale educational surveys such as the National Assessment of Educational Progress. He is a fellow of the Institute of Mathematical Statistics, a member of the board of trustees and the editorial council of the Psychometric Society, and an associate editor and editor-elect of *Psychometrika*. He served on the NRC's Committee on Embedding Common Test Items in State and District Assessments. He is currently a member of the Design and Analysis Committee for the National Assessment of Educational Progress. He has a Ph.D. in statistics from the University of Illinois.

David Klahr is a professor and former head of the Department of Psychology at Carnegie Mellon University. His current research focuses on cognitive development, scientific reasoning, and cognitively based instructional interventions in early science education. His earlier work addressed cognitive processes in such diverse areas as voting behavior, college admissions, consumer choice, peer review, and problem solving. He pioneered the application of information-processing analysis to questions of cognitive development and formulated the first computational models to account for children's thinking processes. He was a member of the NRC's Committee on the Foundations of Assessment. He has a Ph.D. in organizations and social behavior from Carnegie Mellon University.

Ellen Condliffe Lagemann is an education historian and dean of the Harvard Graduate School of Education. She has been a professor of history and education at New York University, taught for 16 years at Teachers College at Columbia University, and served as the president of the Spencer Foundation and the National Academy of Education. She was a member of the NRC's Committee on Scientific Principles in Educational Research. She has an undergraduate degree from Smith College, an M.A. in social studies from Teachers College, and a Ph.D. in history and education from Columbia University.

Barbara Schneider is professor of sociology at the University of Chicago. She is a co-director of the Alfred P. Sloan Center on Parents, Children and Work and the director of the Data Research and Development Center, a new $6 million initiative from Interagency Education Research Initiative. Her current interests include how social contexts, primarily schools and families, influence individuals' interests and actions. She has a Ph.D. from Northwestern University.

Joseph Tobin is a professor in the College of Education at Arizona State

University. Previously he served as a professor in the College of Education at the University of Hawaii. His research interests include educational ethnography, Japanese culture and education, visual anthropology, early childhood education, and children and the media. He was a member of the NRC's Board on International Comparative Studies in Education. He has a Ph.D. in human development from the University of Chicago.

Lisa Towne (*Study Director*) is a senior program officer in the NRC's Center for Education and adjunct instructor of quantitative methods at Georgetown University's Public Policy Institute. She has also worked for the White House Office of Science and Technology Policy and the U.S. Department of Education Planning and Evaluation Service. She has an M.P.P. from Georgetown University.

Tina Winters (*Research Associate*) is a research associate in the NRC's Center for Education. Over the past 10 years, she has worked on a wide variety of education studies at the NRC and has provided assistance for several reports, including *Scientific Research in Education*, *Knowing What Students Know*, and the *National Science Education Standards*.

WORKSHOP SPEAKERS

Diane August is currently an independent consultant as well as a senior research scientist at the Center for Applied Linguistics in Washington, DC. As an educational consultant, she has worked in the areas of literacy, program improvement, evaluation and testing, and federal and state education policy. She has a Ph.D. in education from Stanford University.

Hilda Borko is a professor of education and chair of educational psychology at the School of Education, University of Colorado, Boulder. Her research explores teacher cognition and the process of learning to teach, with an emphasis on changes in novice and experienced teachers' knowledge and beliefs about teaching, learning, and assessment, and their classroom practices. She has a Ph.D. from the University of California, Los Angeles.

Steven Breckler is program director for social psychology at the National Science Foundation (NSF). Since 1995 he has been active in a number of Foundation-wide initiatives, including Learning and Intelligent Systems (LIS), Knowledge and Distributed Intelligence (KDI), the Interagency Education Research Initiative (IERI), and the Children's Research Initiative (CRI). He is currently working to develop a new program to fund Centers for the Science of Learning. He has a Ph.D. from Ohio State University.

Susan Chipman manages the cognitive science program at the U.S. Office of Naval Research, as well as more applied programs in advanced training technology. Previously, she was assistant director of the National Institute of Education, where she was responsible for managing research programs in mathematics education, cognitive development, computers and education, and social influences on learning and development. She has an A.B. in mathematics and M.B.A., A.M., and Ph.D. degrees (the latter in experimental psychology) from Harvard University.

Domenic V. Cicchetti is a senior research scientist of epidemiology and public health in biometry at Yale University School of Medicine. As a psychological methodologist and research collaborator, he has made numerous biostatistical contributions to the development of major clinical instruments in behavioral science and medicine, as well as to the application of state-of-the-art techniques for assessing their psychometric properties. He has B.A., M.A., and Ph.D. degrees from the University of Connecticut.

Louis Danielson is director of the Research to Practice Division in the Office of Special Education Programs (OSEP), U.S. Department of Education. In the field of special education, he has been involved in programs that improve results for students with disabilities. For the past 26 years, he has held leadership roles in OSEP and is currently responsible for the discretionary grants program, including research, technical assistance and dissemination, personnel preparation, technology, and parent training priorities, national evaluation activities, and other major policy-related studies. He has a Ph.D. in educational psychology from Pennsylvania State University.

Kenneth Dodge directs the Center for Child and Family Policy at Duke University. He has studied children's social development and is particularly interested in how chronic violent behavior develops, how it can be prevented in high-risk children, and how communities can implement policies to prevent violence. He has a B.A. from Northwestern University and a Ph.D. in clinical psychology from Duke University.

Edward Hackett is a professor in the Department of Sociology at Arizona State University. He has been an NSF program officer and for 12 years a professor in the Department of Science and Technology Studies at Rensselaer Polytechnic Institute. He has written about peer review, the scientific career, the responsible conduct of research, and the organization and behavior of research groups in science and engineering. He has a B.A. from Colgate University and a Ph.D. from Cornell University.

Milton D. Hakel is the Ohio Board of Regents eminent scholar in industrial and organizational psychology at Bowling Green State University. His research focuses on leadership development, performance appraisal, job analysis and compensation, and employee selection. He is a member of the NRC Board on Testing and Assessment. He has a Ph.D. in psychology from the University of Minnesota.

Teresa Levitin is director of the Office of Extramural Affairs at the National Institute on Drug Abuse (NIDA). Her office houses study sections that review NIDA's medications development, treatment, and services research as well as the agency's career development centers and other special mechanisms. She works with the scientific community to inform them about pertinent policies and procedures as well as to teach research grant-writing skills. She has a Ph.D. in social psychology from the University of Michigan, Ann Arbor.

Penelope Peterson is Eleanor R. Baldwin professor and dean of the School of Education and Social Policy at Northwestern University. Her research interests are literacy and mathematics teaching and learning, student and teacher learning in reform contexts, and educational research, policy, and practice. Since becoming dean, she has led the school in bringing theory and research together with practice to improve learning and teaching in the local educational context. She has a B.S. in psychology and philosophy from Iowa State University and M.A. and Ph.D. degrees in psychological studies in education from Stanford University.

Edward Redish is professor of physics at the University of Maryland, College Park. His research in nuclear theory emphasizes the theory of reactions and the quantum few-body problem. As a nuclear theorist, he served on the National Nuclear Science Advisory Committee and served as chair of the Program Committee for the Indiana Cyclotron. Since 1982 he has been actively involved in the subject of physics education using the computer. He was founder and co-principal investigator of the Maryland University Project in Physics Education and Technology (CUPLE). He is the editor of the physics education supplement to the *American Journal of Physics*. He has an undergraduate degree from Princeton University and a Ph.D. in theoretical nuclear physics from the Massachusetts Institute of Technology.

Finbarr Sloane is program manager for the Interagency Education Research Initiative at the National Science Foundation. In addition to this work, he also assumes the role of program director in the Research on Learning and Education program housed in the Division of Research, Evaluation and Communication. His responsibilities there include oversight of the international study of mathematics and science currently being conducted in 47 countries. He has also sponsored and has oversight over promising technology solutions to teaching and learning in mathematics and science. Sloane has a B.A. in mathematics and sociology from the University College Cork and an M.B.A. from the University of Chicago.

Brent B. Stanfield is the deputy director of the National Institutes of Health (NIH) Center for Scientific Review. Within NIH, he has held positions in the Office of Science Policy, the Division of Intramural Research in the National Institute on Mental Health (NIMH), the Center for Scientific Review (where he helped implement the reorganization of the study sections that review neuroscience grant applications), and the NIMH Office of Science Policy and Program Planning. He has a B.S. in biological sciences from the University of California, Irvine and a Ph.D. in neurobiology from Washington University, St. Louis.

Robert J. Sternberg is IBM professor of psychology and education and director of the Center for the Psychology of Abilities, Competencies, and Expertise at Yale University. The center is dedicated to theory, research, practice, and policy advancing the notion of intelligence as developing expertise—that is, as a construct that is modifiable and capable, to some extent, of development throughout the life span. The central focus of his research is on intelligence, creativity, and wisdom, and he also has studied love and close relationships as well as hate. He has a B.A. (summa cum laude, Phi Beta Kappa,) from Yale University and a Ph.D. from Stanford University.

Grover J. (Russ) Whitehurst is the first director of the Institute of Education Sciences, which was established in the U.S. Department of Education by the Education Sciences Reform Act of 2002. The institute conducts, supports, and disseminates research on education practices that improve academic achievement, statistics on the condition of education in the United States, and evaluations of the effectiveness of federal and other education programs. As director, Whitehurst administers the institute, coordinates its work with that of other federal agencies, and advises the secretary on research, evaluation, and statistics. He has an undergraduate degree from East Carolina University and a Ph.D. in experimental child psychology from the University of Illinois, Urbana-Champaign.